The Ex-Offender's 30/30 Job Solution

Quickly Find a **Lifeboat** *Job Close to Home*

Second Edition

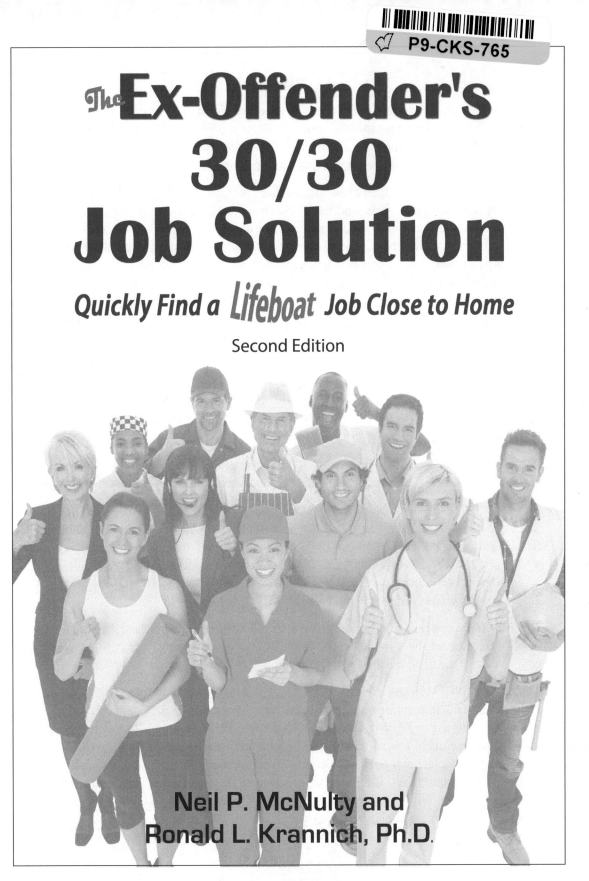

Neil P. McNulty and Ronald L. Krannich, Ph.D.

IMPACT PUBLICATIONS
Manassas Park, VA

ISBNs: 978-1-57023-361-6 (paperback); 978 -1-57023-375-3 (eBook)

Library of Congress: 2015902086

Publisher: For information on Impact Publications, including current and forthcoming publications, authors, press kits, online bookstore, newsletters, downloadable catalogs, and submission requirements, visit the left navigation bar on the front page of the company website:www.impactpublications.com.

Publicity/Rights: For information on publicity, author interviews, and subsidiary rights, contact the Media Relations Department: Tel. 703-361-7300, Fax 703-335-9486, or email: query@impactpublications.com.

Sales/Distribution: All special sales and distribution inquiries should be directed to the publisher: Sales Department, IMPACT PUBLICATIONS, 9104 Manassas Drive, Suite N, Manassas Park, VA 20111-5211, Tel. 703-361-7300, Fax 703-335-9486, or email: query@impactpublications.com. All bookstores sales are handled through Impact's trade distributor: National Book Network, 15200 NBN Way, Blue Ridge Summit, PA 17214, Tel. 1-800-462-6420.

Quantity Discounts: We offer quantity discounts (20-80%) on bulk purchases. Please review our discount schedule for this book on the inside front cover page, at www.impactpublications.com, or contact the Special Sales Department, Tel. 703-361-0255.

The Authors: Neil McNulty is a former Marine Corps infantry officer and president of McNulty Management Group, a staffing and placement firm that pioneered the 30/30 Job Search™: www.mcnultymanagement.com. **Ronald L. Krannich, Ph.D.**, has authored more than 100 books, including many for ex-offenders and people with not-so-hot backgrounds. A former Peace Corps Volunteer and Fulbright Scholar, Ron specializes in producing and distributing career-related products. Neil and Ron also co-authored *The Quick 30/30 Job Solution: Smart Job Search Tips for Surviving Today's New Economy*. The authors can be contacted through the publisher: query@impactpublications.com.

Contents

1

The 30/30 Job Solution for Re-Entry Success

*"Most ex-offenders face important re-entry time and place issues –
quickly find a promising lifeboat job both close to home
and near their parole/probation officer. That requires initiative
in building a resume . . . and burying a rap sheet."*

HOW LONG WILL IT TAKE TO LAND A JOB, and where will you find that job? Those two time and place questions are central to the many challenges facing ex-offenders as they go about the daunting and stressful business of trying to make it in the free world. **Time and place** are of the essence as they must quickly take their own initiative in making many life-altering decisions with outcomes that are anything but certain. After spending so much boring, mind-numbing time in a cage, where they experienced bouts of fear, distrust, and depression, life now comes at them in dizzying speeds, requiring many new decisions and responsibilities. As they soon discover, this new, fascinating, and often scary "life on the outside" is anything but boring!

First and foremost, the **urgency of now** is to find a job and keep it in order to support themselves and stay out of trouble. As we stress throughout this unconventional book, that job often needs to be close to home as well as near their parole or probation officer. For many ex-offenders looking for their first job out, any job will do as long as it provides them with sufficient income to survive on the outside and point them in the promising direction of re-entry success. Put another way, most ex-offenders need to quickly find a **lifeboat job** that will help float their transition to another level.

Why Lifeboat Jobs?

While many employment experts primarily focus on finding ideal jobs – ones their clients do well and enjoy doing – you're different, and thus you require another approach. Re-entry for ex-offenders initially is all about **survival** in the free world without a strong and reliable net. Therefore, we are more concerned that you quickly find a job that helps you support yourself right away as you embark on a new life in the free world. That job should enable you to become stable, self-sufficient, and productive. In short, this book is all about getting that all-important **steppingstone job**. Hopefully that job will also lead to a **satisfying career**. But you need to focus on **first things**

> *Any job can lead to something great if you have the right attitude and work hard.*

first – get a lifeboat job to navigate some choppy waters ahead and avoid drowning in a sea of "must do's." It's all about **taking initiative** (something that may have been killed while doing time in a cage), acquiring important knowledge, and using wise reality-based strategies for reshaping your future.

In today's challenging economy, we increasingly focus on what we call a lifeboat job. Such a job may well become your key to long-term re-entry success. Handled properly, it should give your life both **purpose** and **direction**. Better still, it will help you avoid that **vicious cycle of recidivism** that too often plagues the lives of many ex-offenders and reflects a failed criminal justice system.

Let's begin by clarifying what we mean by a lifeboat job. It's one you need to find NOW – not six months down the road – in order to keep yourself financially afloat. It's essentially a survival, stop-gap, or bridge job that may or may not lead to a rewarding career. It's not one you should agonize over for long. Just take it, and get on with your life. After all, better days lie ahead for those who welcome opportunities and respond accordingly. You can always change jobs after you get settled in, establish meaningful routines, and build your resume in the process of burying your rap sheet!

While many lifeboat jobs are dead-end jobs, others lead to meaningful careers. Indeed, this book should assist you in finding "good" lifeboat jobs – those with a promising future – rather than "bad" lifeboat jobs – those that go nowhere, may depress your future, or lead to trouble.

As you journey through life, you soon discover that there are both **seasons and purposes in life** that are subject to changes that may or may not be within your control. Let's face it. Sometimes personal circumstances, such as your incarceration, dictate that you must find a job that may not particularly appeal to you, but it's a job that will support you as well as contribute to your long-term freedom. Such jobs give you a secure financial footing so that you can take care of your basic housing, clothing, food, transportation, and other essential daily living needs. While such jobs may turn out to be very satisfying and eventually lead to career advancement, they at least give you a paycheck in exchange for your labor. Understandably, you need to quickly develop a steady income stream in order to survive, and hopefully do well, on the outside. In the process, you should grow into the job by acquiring new skills, becoming accomplished, and getting promoted. Best of all, you'll turn that lifeboat into a positive long-term career!

Transformative Jobs for Ex-Offenders

Ex-offenders know all too well the importance of lifeboat jobs and survival on the outside. Being released from prison or jail without money, a job, or family support, and facing immediate housing, clothing, food, medical, and transportation needs – as well as probation and parole reporting requirements – they need to quickly land a job near where they live.

Not all lifeboat jobs are dead-end jobs. Indeed, many are **transformative** – they put your life on an unexpected journey to somewhere you never thought possible but extremely rewarding nonetheless. In fact, no matter what you've done, dead-end job or otherwise, any job – even digging ditches or delivering pizzas – can lead to something great if you have the **right attitude, work hard, and persist**. Just think about it for a moment. All companies, no matter what service they provide or product they produce, have people who own them, run them, make money, and have a real career. Many ex-offenders who now run major companies once started out at the very bottom. Take, for example, David Koch (author of ***Slaying the Dragon***) who established a Fortune 500 company and sold it for millions after doing serious prison time. Then there's actor Robert Downey, Jr., who seemingly conquered his drug demons and became today's highest paid actor. The list goes on and on with Martha Stewart, Tim Allen, 50 Cent, Wesley Snipes, Don King, Lil Wayne, James Brown, and Mike Tyson. Not all conquered their demons, but they did time and survived against many odds. Along the less visible celebrity route, you'll find restaurant chain owners who started their careers by delivering pizzas – they were ex-offenders. You'll find owners of major construction companies who began with a shovel in their hands digging ditches under a hot sun – and they were ex-offenders. The main difference is these people worked harder than others and had the right attitude for success. And that's what you need to do. This book will show you how to find good lifeboat jobs – ones that lead to a career if you work hard and have the right **attitude**. For many ex-offenders, attitude is something they need to work on.

Unfortunately, few people know how to find good lifeboat jobs. Many waste a great deal of time looking for jobs in all the wrong places and then eventually settle for hard-labor, low-paying, and unstable day laborer jobs. Such jobs may in fact be impediments to long-term survival on the outside. Your goal should be to land a good job with a promising future.

The Ex-Offender Lifeboat Experience

Most ex-offenders expect to face difficulties in landing a job given their criminal backgrounds. After all, employers are not social experiments. Why would they want to take a chance and hire a known ex-offender? Regardless of what you may think of yourself – real or delusional – isn't it risky business to hire someone with your background?

Since most employers ask questions about criminal backgrounds (*Have you ever been convicted of a crime or felony?*) and many conduct background checks on everything from employment record (*Is it stable and progressive?*) to credit history (*What is your FICO score?*), today there are few places ex-offenders can hide from their red flag backgrounds.

Not surprisingly, a disproportionate number of ex-offenders already gravitate to lifeboat jobs. These are basically unattractive, dead-end jobs few people want. Such jobs tend to have the following characteristics:

- experience high worker turnover
- pay low wages and salaries
- offer few benefits
- require limited specialized skills
- ask few background questions
- require no pre-employment testing
- are physically demanding
- represent part-time work
- may require a lengthy commute
- lack employment stability

No wonder these are low-paying, high-cost jobs with little or no future. Many of these jobs, which may require a long commute and hard work, are often more of a financial burden than a benefit. After a while, you may discover that you can't afford to continue in such a job. You need to move up the lifeboat ladder to find a good lifeboat job that's more responsive to your income needs and interests.

Ex-offenders typically take these high-turnover lifeboat jobs that require little customer contact, offer low wages and few benefits, and can be physically demanding:

- day laborers/handymen
- construction
- lawn maintenance
- cleaning/janitorial
- roofers
- moving services
- manufacturing
- warehousing
- food processors/preparers
- waiters/waitresses

Many restaurants, for example, have annual turnover rates of 90 percent or more – perfect places for seeking lifeboat jobs.

But there are many other lifeboat jobs with a more promising future available for those who know how to find such jobs. Ron outlines many such jobs in his recent book ***Best Jobs for Ex-Offenders: 101 Opportunities to Jump-Start Your New Life***. Neil, who created the innovative 30/30 Placement Program, has helped thousands of people find jobs using his 30/30 Job Search™ techniques. Indeed, the 30/30 program is one many people can use to secure a lifeboat job. It's especially relevant to anyone with a stable work history and marketable skills who is looking for employment in a difficult and challenging economy. It also can be adapted to ex-offenders with less than stable work histories who need to quickly find employment close to home.

> *You should be able to find a lifeboat job within 30 days and within 30 miles of where you live.*

In the following pages, our mission is to make sure you expand the range of your job search as well as use a variety of smart guerrilla strategies and techniques to land a job based upon Neil's 30/30 program. If you learn the key job search lessons in the following chapters and put them into practice, you should be able to find a lifeboat job within 30 days and within 30 miles of where you live. Best of all, you'll go a long way toward jump-starting your life on the outside and securing a better future for both you and your family, because you found a "good" lifeboat job!

Find a Job Within 30 Days

As an ex-offender, you need to quickly find a job upon release. If you've participated in a transitional work experience, such as a halfway house involving subsidized job training and wage-paid temporary work with wrap-around supports and services, you may be well positioned to find a job upon release. Indeed, many ex-offenders who are fortunate to get such transitional work experience with government agencies, nonprofit organizations, or local businesses

> *Your goal should be to create an employment record and resume that is more compelling than your criminal record and rap sheet.*

– especially in construction, manufacturing, food preparation, hospitality, printing, transportation, warehousing, and distribution industries – may be able to quickly find employment upon release. Such individuals are able to create a recent work record that appeals to employers who might otherwise only focus on the individual's prison record or rap sheet.

Your goal should be to create an **employment record and resume** that are more compelling than your **criminal record and rap sheet**. This record and resume should indicate that you have marketable skills and that you will become a productive and loyal employee with a stable work history.

In the following pages we outline proven strategies that have helped thousands of individuals find lifeboat jobs within 30 days. Organized as a program of unconventional job hunter guerrilla tactics, our techniques quickly put job seekers in contact with employers who want to hire them. It is a relatively brief, streamlined process, and leaves out many topics normally included in most job search books.

Let's get started with this process by identifying two jobs you've had, including any transitional work experiences, that would indicate to an employer that you have useful, **marketable skills** and would be a **dependable employee** in lieu of a stable record of employment:

Job	Marketable Skills
1. _____	_____
2. _____	_____

Get Employed Within 30 Miles From Home

More and more individuals want to find employment close to home. Given the high costs of commuting long distances to work, today's job seekers prefer finding a job within an easy 20- to 30-minute commute. In fact, many people are willing to take a lower paying job that is close to home than a higher paying job that requires a lengthy commute. Spending two to three hours each day commuting 100 to 150 miles roundtrip may cost more than $50.00 a day in fuel, tolls, maintenance, and parking fees – recurring expenses few people with limited budgets can sustain for long. Add to this the lost time and high stress associated with such lengthy commutes and you probably have a recipe for an unhappy worklife and future unemployment!

Many ex-offenders have little choice in this matter. For them, a long commute can be very costly in terms of both time and money. Some lack adequate public or private transportation to get to job sites. Added to these costs is the need to stay close to one's probation and parole officer. As ex-offenders soon discover in the free world, their choices tend to be limited and freedom can be costly! For them, our innovative 30/30 job solution offers great promise for jump-starting their life on the outside.

Let's start thinking about your essential employment needs by focusing on your housing, income, and commuting needs each day:

My new address (city and street): _____

Minimum amount I need to make
(hourly wage or yearly salary): _____

Maximum miles I can afford to
commute to work each day: _____

30/30 Success on Your Own and With Assistance

The following pages are designed to help you clarify exactly what it is you need to do in order to land a good lifeboat job. Filled with insider tips and techniques, the remaining five chapters and three appendices will show you how to overcome barriers to employment by targeting specific employers and jobs the 30/30 way.

While most of the material in the remainder of this book is based upon Neil's experiences as a 30/30 placement professional who works with both job seekers and employers, especially transitioning military personnel, we've adapted his techniques for conducting an unconventional re-entry job search on your own. For more information on Neil's 30/30 approach, please see our companion volume – *The Quick 30/30 Job Solution: Smart Job Search Tips for Surviving Today's New Economy* (see page 122).

We're confident that if you perform the actions prescribed in this book, you'll be very successful in landing a job within 30 days and within 30 miles of your home! That new lifeboat job may also open doors to a very satisfying long-term career. At least that is our hope as you fully transition into the free world with a combination of purpose, meaning, and joy. When you do that, you will be truly **free at last**!

2

Three Unconventional Principles That Can Work for You

"Employment opportunities are everywhere – you just need to know how to best link your talents to employers' needs."

THE PROGRAM OUTLINED IN the following pages is often referred as "job hunter guerrilla tactics." These are **unconventional job finding methods** designed to help you outsmart other job seekers who use conventional approaches – those who literally "follow the rules" on how to find a job. Unfortunately, many of the so-called "rules" are also job search myths that can take you down the wrong path to job search failure. In today's economy, you need to literally **think outside the box** by using many of the unique approaches outlined in this book.

It's Now Okay to Break the Rules

As an ex-offender, you know about breaking and following rules. Like many other people, you broke a rule somewhere and paid a price for doing so. Your reward/sentence – more mindless control rules surrounding your cage behavior! But job hunting is one activity where breaking the rules can be a good thing for both you and employers. Indeed, when you follow our unconventional job search strategies, having 30/30 "street smarts" can pay off big for you. The trick is in knowing which rules you should break and which rules you shouldn't break. This book will teach you the difference.

Become Your Own Campaign Manager

Like a candidate running for office, you become your own "Campaign Manager" (CM) within a specific geographic area where you hope to be "elected" (hired). You target supporters (employers) with specific information about how your talents can best benefit them. Key supporters decide to bring you on board to help solve their problems.

Everything in our 30/30 job search program centers on three job search principles:

1. Talent Intersecting Opportunity
2. Talent and Geography
3. 30-Mile Placement

7

As we emphasize throughout this book, you must learn, internalize, and believe in these principles in order to make them work for you.

Talent Intersecting Opportunity (TIO) Principle

Our 30/30 program is based upon this first important principle – **Talent Intersecting Opportunity (TIO)**. This principle goes beyond just identifying job openings and responding to them in a conventional manner. Here's how this principle works:

> *If a job hunter communicates his or her marketable skills and a desirable pattern of work behavior to enough key decision-makers, as well as initiates effective follow-up actions, he or she will receive employment offers regardless of announced openings or current economic conditions.*

In other words, you must take initiative in marketing your **talents** (skills and abilities) to individuals who have a need for your skills and who have the power to hire you. While they may or may not have an announced job opening, they will hire you because once they meet you, they recognize that you are the one who will **add value** to their company or operations. You are seen as an important **asset** for expanding their business.

Employment opportunities exist everywhere and at all times; job "openings" do not.

The TIO Principle is an important truth that will serve you well throughout your working life. Indeed, your career and livelihood will never be endangered as long as you have marketable skills and perform well in your work. Regardless of technological advances and the increasing use of social media in the job search/recruitment process, people hire people only after they meet them face-to-face.

"Talent" must intersect "opportunity"; however, "opportunity" does not necessarily mean advertised "job openings." Employment opportunities exist everywhere and at all times; job "openings" do not. Therefore, you should always think in terms of **opening doors of opportunity** – not just responding to announced job openings or vacancies.

Always remember that employers have **needs**, many of which are never announced as job openings. Your job is to uncover employment opportunities by marketing your skills and abilities to potential employers. That's where your talent intersects opportunity. When it does, you'll progress from employment opportunities to employment offers.

Using this program, you'll learn the fastest and most effective ways to make this principle work for you – intersect your talent with opportunity. You'll become a Campaign Manager for your own 30/30 job search.

The number of such opportunities you must uncover in order to receive a job offer is not high – usually between four and six. Following our 30/30 process, this means you'll probably receive a job offer after meeting only four to six key people. You'll need to carefully follow each step of this process in order for it to work to your advantage.

Let's start thinking about putting this TIO Principle into practice by identifying three of your **major talents** (skills or abilities) that might intersect with opportunities that you locate with potential employers. In listing your talents, try to be as specific as possible. For example, if you are trained in electronics and can repair equipment, put down "can repair electronic equipment." If you are not skilled in a trade, but are an excellent writer, you can put down "can write and edit material in a timely manner." If you have no skills at all, but are very physically fit from working out, it is even okay to put down "am very physically strong" (some companies want physically impressive people, such as moving companies, gymnasiums, construction companies, and security companies). You get the picture...the key is to think hard about what you can do for someone which they might be willing to pay you to do. Now go ahead and list your three **major talents** desired by employers:

1. _____

2. _____

3. _____

At the same time, identify your three most important **work behaviors** (such as getting to work on time, following instructions, getting along with co-workers, taking initiative, dependability, etc.) that potential employers might find most attractive. Keep in mind that employers are looking for a stable work history along with key skills and abilities. If you think you lack a stable work history because of your red flag background, identify three other work behaviors that might compensate for your lack of work stability:

1. _____

2. _____

3. _____

Now, state how your talent might best intersect with opportunities you identify through our 30/30 process. State it in the following talent-to-opportunity form:

My ability to _____ *will be discovered by an*
(specify key talent and/or workplace behavior)

employer who will hire me to _____
(specify an opportunity – something that adds value to an employer)

Talent and Geography (TAG) Principle

The second key principle of our 30/30 program is **Talent and Geography (TAG)**. This principle recognizes the fact that **talent usually prefers working close to home** rather than relocating to another community or making long daily commutes to work:

Today the vast majority of workers place far more importance on the geographic location of an opportunity than on the importance of an opportunity for their career advancement. Simply put, they prefer working close to home.

Similar to the great real estate principle of location, location, location, today's job seekers are more location-specific than ever before. Indeed, people prefer living and working where they and their families want to live. For many job seekers, finding job opportunities is like real estate – it's all about location, location, location!

Neil discovered this important principle in the 1980s. A former Marine, he joined one of the most prestigious and successful search and placement companies – Management Recruiters International – where he specialized in recruiting and placing junior military officers (JMOs). Corporations aggressively recruit JMOs because of their leadership, maturity, and experience. But Neil soon noticed that something very significantly had changed with these highly sought-after recruits: Most JMOs said they would go wherever opportunities arose, but when it came time to take a job involving relocation, many would not make the move. Instead, they preferred staying in their current location. As a result, Neil shifted his placement focus toward finding opportunities located only in the desired geographic locations of JMOs.

Today, quality of life is more important than ever for most people – surpassing career and financial growth.

Neil's specialty quickly became his ability to place junior officers with companies located within 30 miles of their favorite geographic locations. This eliminated relocation worries for hiring companies and relocation concerns for the placed JMOs and their families. It also relieved many "fall-off" (failure to report for work) concerns for recruiters because the officers placed were excited about the locations they were going to.

In 1994 Neil opened his own placement firm that specialized in placing candidates – not just JMOs – only in their preferred geographic locations. Thus, the 30/30 concept and program was born. It's now used by many staffing and placement firms for geographically targeted placements. Even during recessions, economic downturns, and wars, the 30/30 methods have consistently resulted in hires. While many search and placement firms have come and gone, 30/30 firms continue to be successful because they operate according to the TAG Principle.

Today, **quality of life issues** are more important than ever. People live and work where they desire most to live and work, and many will gladly pay the career or financial price for being able to do so. There are, of course, exceptions to this principle. In fact, you may be willing to go anywhere for work. But chances are you're more selective – you want to work near where you currently live or at least within a short (under 30 minutes) commute. Unlike many other individuals, you also may face legal restrictions on where you can find employment – live in a place that is near a parole/probation officer.

30-Mile Placement Principle

We call our third and final principle the **30-Mile Placement Principle**. This is a geographic preference principle:

> *Except when facing highly unusual economic, geographic, or occupational circumstances, when using the correct approach, almost every type of talented person can*

30-Mile Placement Principle

Within 30 miles of any point on the map are employment
opportunities which fit almost every type of person.

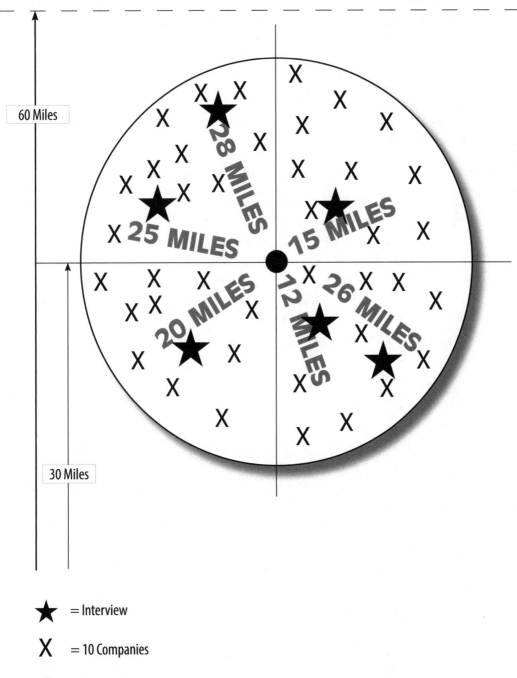

60 Miles

28 MILES

25 MILES

15 MILES

20 MILES

12 MILES

26 MILES

30 Miles

★ = Interview

X = 10 Companies

● = Center of Search Zone

find satisfying employment somewhere within a 30-mile radius of any medium-sized population center within the continental United States.

A 30-mile radius represents an area that is commonly referred to as a "local job market." This is the maximum one-way distance most people will travel to work. It also represents a minimum-sized geographic area where a sufficient number of potential employers can be found for targeting a successful job search. The figure on page 11 illustrates this important principle.

While almost any kind of talented person should be able to find employment within 30 miles of any medium-sized (150,000 minimum population) community, this does not mean that 30/30 will not work within rural areas. In fact, this program works quite well in remote areas. It simply works best near population centers of at least 150,000 people, which are medium-sized cities.

Old Myths and New Zones of Opportunities (ZOOs)

How many times have you heard the following statements, or considered these thoughts, when looking for a job?

"A serious job hunter is willing to relocate to where the best jobs can be found."
"I can't find a job, because there aren't enough good jobs in this area. Why should I spend time looking for something in this wasteland?"

"So many companies are laying people off around here . . . I might as well forget about ever finding anything worthwhile here."

"None of the career websites has appropriate listings for people with my background and located where we're moving."

"No one wants to hire an ex-offender."

"Everyone says that since my parole board says I cannot relocate, I'll face a very long job search."

These statements and thoughts are largely myths about job finding approaches. For some job seekers, these myths – especially *"I can't find a job"* – also represent excuses or rationalizations for not taking actions that would result in job interviews and offers. Indeed, such myths dissuade many people from taking effective actions that could result in a 30/30 job.

The good news is this: almost **all companies**, large and small, at **all locations**, and at almost **all times**, exhibit the following internal employment characteristics and dynamics that lead to hiring more people, such as yourself. Most have this combination of positions, needs, problems, and goals:

1. presently open positions
2. soon-to-be open positions
3. unsatisfied needs
4. unsolved problems
5. a leader's vision for the organization that requires new people and capabilities

Viewed from the perspective of a smart and assertive job seeker, these characteristics and dynamics are indicators of possible **employment opportunities**. Viewed from our 30/30 perspective, such potential employment opportunities are **Zones of Opportunities**, or **ZOOs** for short, that argue well for our 30/30 intervention strategies for finding a job which may or may not have been formally announced or advertised.

As we stress throughout this book, your goal should be to intersect or link your talents with these different Zones of Opportunities by meeting with potential employers in at least six companies located in your targeted geographic area.

> *You need to link your talents with different Zones of Opportunities (ZOOs) by meeting with six potential employers.*

The Widespread Reality of ZOOs

Our concept of ZOOs is a powerful tool for finding a 30/30 job. Somewhat abstract, nonetheless, this concept becomes a reality once you target your job search and take actions that put you in the midst of ZOOs where you will meet with key decision-makers and persuade them to acquire your talents.

If you want to intersect your talents with ZOOs, you must really believe that ZOOs can be found nearly everywhere. Perhaps you find this difficult to believe since you've not had experience in conducting a job search using an expansive ZOOs approach. Trust us on this critical concept, which will become central to your 30/30 job search. Whatever you do from this point on, you must change the way you view the job market or you will have difficulty finding ZOOs. Worst of all, you'll fulfill your own negative expectations and create a negative self-fulfilling prophecy.

The following story involving Neil in his previous professional life illustrates the concept of ZOOs and how pervasive and important they can be for "survival":

> When I was a Marine, my unit underwent wilderness survival training. This training was conducted in a forest classroom, and we were seated in a semicircle on the ground. The instructor began the class by asking us how much "food" we thought was within 50 feet of where we were seated. Some of the members of my unit had been Boy Scouts when they were young and, as such, had received training in how to find food in the woods. They told the instructor there were probably some plants in the area with roots that were edible, also that they could set traps to snare rabbits, rodents, or snakes by using such items as boot laces and belts from our uniform trousers.
>
> The instructor agreed, but then stated that those methods were much more advanced than what was necessary, especially if we were alone in the woods and needed to keep moving. He then reached down and pulled up a clod of grass. Holding the clod of grass, he pointed out that he now had in his hands *"three earthworms, four small pill-shaped bugs, and something that looks like a cricket."* He noted how all of these "critters" were edible, were full of protein, could be popped into the mouth, and how there is never any reason for anyone to starve in the forest because *"Food in the forest is never more than a pull away!"* He quickly changed our thinking regarding food.

ZOOs are the same. Instead of reaching down and pulling up a clump of grass to uncover food, a job hunter should learn how to reach out and contact key decision-makers. That Marine instructor was not worried about some insect jumping out of that clump of grass and biting him, nor was he concerned about disturbing the natural order of insects. Similarly, you should not worry about human beings "biting" you when you call them, email them, or write to them regarding how you can add value to their organizations. In fact, many employers want to hear from thoughtful individuals who share their concerns and who might help solve their problems.

> *Using our 30/30 program, you will rarely, if ever, annoy anyone when contacting them.*

Don't allow the word "contact" to frighten you. You will learn that one of the most important aspects of our 30/30 program is how you will rarely, if ever, annoy or bother anyone when contacting them. We address this issue later when we examine how best to approach key decision-makers who have the power to hire.

Finding Your Zones of Opportunity (ZOO)

If you have any doubts about the abundance and importance of ZOOs, ask yourself these seven questions:

1. Within 30 miles of where you live, or where you are relocating to, how many total companies or organizations, big and small, do you think there are? Hundreds? Thousands? (HINT: look at business listings in the telephone book)

2. Would you agree that each company or organization is a potential employer?

3. How many of these employers do not seek improved performance?

4. How many of these employers have no unsolved problems?

5. How many of these employers have no unmet needs?

6. How many of these employers lack a vision for the future of their companies, or for their departments if in a large organization?

7. How many of these employers would give an ex-offender a chance if the ex-offender showed a strong ability and desire to bring value to their organization?

Today's workplaces are very mobile, with people leaving companies, on average, every three to five years. Knowing this, how many people do you think are in the process of trying to change jobs, either openly or confidentially, within 30 miles of any mid-sized metropolitan area? The conservative answer is hundreds. How many are leaving jobs that you might find satisfying? Unless you are very selective, the answer is many.

To help you better visualize the reality of ZOOs, let's start mapping the ground game, which will become the nuts-and-bolts of your potentially richly rewarding 30/30 job search. Is there, for example, a large office building located in the place where you want to work? If so, go on a mapping website (for starters, try maps.google.com) and look at its satellite picture. If that building contains multiple companies, you are looking at a building with many types of businesses and people, and many people **who are**

secretly trying to change jobs. Also, unless you have a very unusual profession, the chances are that **at least one** ideal opportunity (remember, an "opportunity" does not necessarily mean an "opening") exists somewhere within its walls right now. In fact, a skilled user of 30/30 techniques could set a goal of becoming employed in that very building, and would have a fair chance of accomplishing it!

> *You need to visualize organizations as having fluid environments with unlimited job opportunities.*

Learn to see all organizations for what they really are: **fluid environments with unlimited present and potential employment opportunities**, or ZOOs, and with all types of people coming and going constantly – senior executives, middle managers, junior managers, professionals, office staffers, blue-collar workers, and everyone else who adds value to the company or business. Once you begin seeing organizations in these terms – put on your ZOO eyes – you'll be better prepared to organize your 30/30 ground game with a clear vision.

What Employers Want

Many employers would interview and hire an outstanding person right now if one came along who showed they would **add value** to their operations. Organizational leaders are like coaches of sports teams: they are always scouting out for the next star, even when the present "roster" is full. All businesses and business leaders have Zones of Opportunities (ZOOs), even those going bankrupt, experiencing tough times, or laying people off! Businesses with problems need new people with fresh ideas in order to change direction. They represent ZOOs.

If you can learn how to intersect your talent with the ZOOs, you will be on the road to success. Our 30/30 program will show you the most effective ways to do that.

Key Program Elements

Let's turn to some of the key elements or principles that define our 30/30 job search program and which provide the necessary structure for the remainder of this book. Knowing these elements and how they relate to one another should give you confidence in this program and get you thinking and believing in the proper terms regarding the abundance of opportunities that exist everywhere and during all economic conditions.

The 30/30 Job Search™ Defined

> "The 30/30 Job Search™ is a job hunting program used for finding satisfying employment located within 30 miles of the job hunter's ideal geographic location, and the employment should be found within 30 days of beginning the program."

Our 30/30 job search program will not be successful for every job hunter who uses it. Its overall (all users) documented success rate is 73 percent and, frankly, most failures are usually due to the user, not the program. Some 30/30 users will not be diligent and will take longer than 30 days to find satisfying employment. Others will not perform the work required for success. Still others will be offered satisfying employment very early on but turn the offer down because it happened so fast, only to realize too late that the opportunity was the best opportunity. There are many factors which contribute to this program's success or failure. Nonetheless, if you perform the work as prescribed, you have a very good chance for success. However, keep in mind that for 30 days you will be **very** busy performing the required functions if you truly desire success.

30/30 Activities and Phases

The 30/30 program consists of three activities conducted over three phases:

1. Research and Planning (Phase I)
2. Action (Phase II)
3. Getting Hired and Reporting for Work (Phase III)

Here's our projected time frame for successfully completing the three 30/30 activities and phases:

Activity	Phase/Time
1. Research and Planning	I (Days 1-4)
2. Action	II (Days 5-8)
3. Getting Hired/Reporting for Work	III (Days 9-30)

PHASE I: Research and Planning. Includes assembling a complete Campaign Plan. This should require no more than four days to accomplish. The Campaign Plan is your systematic "map" to interviews and job offers. To construct this plan, you will:

- Use software, web pages, directories, and the telephone book.

- Develop your Contact List – a list of companies and the key decision-makers or leaders at those companies.

- Identify companies by products, services, size, sales volume, address, numbers of employees, and geography, but you will not perform "in-depth" research.

- Research key leaders and learn where they live.

- Plan your pursuit of advertised openings and "opportunity leads" by using the "Candidate Contrived Coincidence" tactic.

- Create a "chronological resume" if you have been incarcerated for one year or less; create a "functional resume" if your incarceration has been longer than one year.

- Write a "baseline" presentation of your profile.

- Prepare responses to predictable employer questions.

Your completed plan will ideally consist of a list of up to 150 of the best companies in your Search Zone.

PHASE II: Action. This involves the execution of your Campaign Plan. This should require no more than five days to complete. You will:

- Use a multi-pronged approach to contact the companies and key leaders on your Contact List.

- Work in efficient "time blocks" and perform the tasks you planned in Phase I.

- Leave voicemail messages which will be heard.

- Send emails that will be read.

- Write letters which will be answered.

- Use the "Candidate Contrived Coincidence" technique to pursue advertised openings.

- Schedule meetings with potential employers.

Above all, you will initiate and develop friendly, cordial, yet businesslike relationships with all whom you encounter, while never losing focus on your purpose: to intersect your talent with opportunity.

PHASE III: Getting Hired. This includes going on interviews and finalizing employment at competitive compensation. This should require no more than 20 days to complete. You will:

- Prepare for interviews, especially study and apply the interview principles outlined in Appendix A.

- Rehearse your answers to possible questions until you sound and appear confident, effective, extroverted, and conversational, yet not sound "programmed" or rehearsed. See Appendix B for 100+ sample interview questions. Interviewing techniques that are not included in Appendix A should not be used.

- Avoid being "over prepared" or trying to have answers for every possible question. You don't want to appear "too smooth."

- Close your interviews by scheduling follow-up appointments using the "Interview Closing Sequence" (ICS) scheduling technique.

- Write thank-you notes using the 30/30 method and "pre-close" regarding salary and compensation, but only at the right time.

- Do not ask for more than two minor changes to any negotiated job offer.

- Accept an offer immediately if it is what you asked for. Resist any "let me think it over" situations, thus avoiding possible hard feelings on the employer's part (or withdrawal of the offer!).

- Promptly perform any pre-employment tasks and report for work on the agreed date.

3

Communication Technology for 30/30 Success

"An effective job search requires smart and unconventional communication strategies targeted toward those who actually have the power to hire."

T HE INTERNET, COMPUTERS, and technology in general provide powerful job hunting tools. However, except for those who have access to our 30/30 program, few job seekers understand how to properly use this technology in a job search. Not surprisingly, many job seekers remain technologically savvy but job search dumb! Indeed, they may understand how technology works, but they use it poorly in finding a job. After all, **finding a job is by definition a very personal face-to-face experience** involving such key nonverbal concepts as "likability."

Using Job Search Technology

Technology is often promoted as the key to job search success – a job can be found just through a few clicks of a mouse. In reality, job hunters engage in wishful thinking when they answer online job advertisements by following the online instructions, emailing a resume to a corporate website, posting a resume on a "job board," or emailing a corporate executive without using that person's "real" email address. Used as advertised and advocated by some so-called job search experts, such technology creates an **illusion** of job hunting progress.

On the other hand, many ex-offenders are unfamiliar with today's job search technology. Locked in a cage, most have been living behind a fire wall – no Internet access – lacking sufficient knowledge and skills to conduct an online job search. Accordingly, they may be more open to useful tips on how to best use this technology in a job search based on our 30/30 concepts.

The Illusion of Making Progress

Despite the fact that millions of job seekers post their resumes online and respond to online job listings (the Internet equivalent of the traditional classified newspaper ad), fewer than 20 percent of job seekers ever get interviews or offers by using this job search method. Worst of all, many job seekers spend 90 percent of their job search time looking for jobs online! They regard their hours of online job search experience as working hard at finding a job. It's the classic "looking in all the wrong places" approach to finding a job.

Neil's many years of placement experience confirms the relative ineffectiveness of conducting an online job search:

> *In my entire placement career, I have spoken with only a handful of people who have found a job by emailing a resume in response to an online job posting, corporate website, "job board," or career transition website.*

An "illusion of success" occurs when such job seekers believe they are making job search progress. Engaged in lots of online "busy work," some tech-savvy job seekers receive responses to their online applications. However, most such responses come from recruiters and business people who source candidates online to fill jobs unrelated to the advertised positions; some responses come from employment scam operations. Most often the end result is the same – no new job located where you want it to be. The reason for this is obvious, and it is the same problem that has always existed: too many applicants. Companies once believed that technology would help to quickly narrow the applicant field. In reality, it had the opposite effect. Instead of hundreds of "snail mail" resumes, employers now receive **thousands** of online applications. Even the best resume-screening software is ineffective because so many job seekers know how to use keywords to bypass screening tools.

Many job seekers feel they are making progress by conducting an online job search. But few ever get interviews or job offers based on such online efforts.

E-cruiting Realities

Neil was once shown the electronic "in-basket" to an advertised position a company had run on its corporate web page and also on a major online recruiting website. The mailbox had over 1,200 "pre-screened" resumes in it, and this company used the latest resume-screening software. The recruiter admitted that emails are **randomly** selected for opening until at least five potentially qualified candidates are found. The rest would receive computer-generated rejection letters. Simply put, applicants who apply for positions online have about as much of a chance of gaining an interview as winning the lottery. Such is the norm in the world of "e-cruiting."

The 30/30 program primarily uses technology for gathering information, researching, planning, and for strengthening your relationships during interview processes by emailing communications at effective points in time. Email also is used for establishing initial contact with potential employers, but it's done in conjunction with voicemail and postal mail. Online advertisements are pursued as "job leads" and answered only after more creative methods of getting an interview have been unsuccessful. While business-to-business sales software is recommended for 30/30, it's unnecessary since this program can be effectively implemented by using such "low-tech" tools as a telephone and telephone directory!

Software and 30/30

For the best results with the 30/30 program, and to stay within the program's timetables established for each phase, you should use a computer and basic telephone directory software. Simple software, which lists the telephone numbers and addresses of the companies and people who are listed in the telephone book where you desire to work, is ideal. It would also be helpful if the software identified companies by products and/or services, sales volume, and number of employees. Beyond these few functions, there is no need for added sophistication.

Our 30/30 program uses the Internet, email, telephone, voicemail, and postal mail – a powerful combination of high- and low-tech tools for job search success.

In fact, the simpler the software, the better for this program. The best program comes from Hoovers.com, but it's very expensive. You may be able to access it through a public library. You'll find many inexpensive or free "off-the-shelf" software programs that will work well with our program. However, after experimenting with several programs, we recommend using Manta (www.Manta.com) for identifying small businesses. The good news is that that the online version is free to any user.

Whether you use Manta or other resources, you will probably need a program to complete Phase I, "Research and Planning," within four days and stay on a 30-day target timeline for 30/30 success. Nonetheless, such software is not necessary for this program. If you do not use software, however, you must have access to the business and residential phone books for the geographic area(s) you are targeting. These are easily found online, as every telephone book in the United States is on the Internet. Simply "google" the name of the town you're targeting, plus the words "telephone book," and a variety of resources will appear. You do this by typing www.google.com into your computer's address section or browser (or the browser of a computer at your local library). Then in the Google search bar type the name of the town or city you are targeting, plus the words "telephone book," and a variety of resources will appear.

Telephone Voicemail – Your Best Job Hunting Tool

For its first 30 years, the job placement industry used only one tool: the telephone. There were no voicemail, email, text messaging, or even fax machines. A placement professional had only three possible ways to arrange interviews for candidates: the telephone, regular mail (now often called "snail mail"), and personal visits with companies. The last two, "snail mail" and personal visits, were never effective unless the placement consultant had first spoken on the telephone with the company. Placement consultants who relied upon anything other than the telephone usually failed at the business. Highly successful placement industry professionals were masters at telephone selling then, as they are today.

You are not going to become a "placement professional" with this program, so you do not need to learn to "sell" on the telephone. In fact, you don't need to use the telephone at all! However, for the fastest results with 30/30 (or any job hunting program) the telephone is the best tool. That's because a phone call to the right person at the right time can result in an **immediate** interview . . . and possibly **an immediate job offer**. Also, for this program, you only need to communicate "effectively" over the telephone. "Communicate effectively" is defined as "speaking on the phone with (real or fake) confidence." You can learn to do that by disciplining yourself to get on the telephone. For most people, it's usually only the first few calls which are nerve-wracking.

Using the telephone, especially voicemail, will be central to your success. Voicemail is the simplest, safest, and best tool for finding opportunities.

Job hunting programs everywhere teach the importance of learning to use the telephone for networking and making contacts with leaders who have the power to hire. To most job hunters, the telephone is a frightening instrument, and they will do anything to avoid making calls, because they fear interrupting the leader, embarrassing themselves in some way, appearing weak, or being rejected.

We know from a quarter century of calling leaders that they rarely, if ever, become irritated when telephoned by job hunters, **even if interrupted by the calls**. Most are flattered and are happy to assist.

The telephone really is the most effective tool for job hunting, but it is the least used. This program will teach you the painless way to use the telephone, and that involves the smart use of voicemail.

Neil designed this program around the telephone, but in such a way that you'll never have to worry about the negatives of using the phone. Your fear of using the telephone will become significantly reduced when you discover how easy it is to leave voicemail messages with leaders.

If you do as you are about to be trained, you will rarely struggle with a gatekeeper, interrupt a meeting, embarrass yourself, or be rejected. That's because you will rarely speak with anyone who does not wish to speak with you. They will **return your call** from the messages you leave on voicemail. Even though asking for and speaking directly with a leader is always best for success, you may have a deep fear of doing that. Voicemail is the answer.

Voicemail is the simplest, safest, and best technological tool for finding opportunities. With voicemail messaging, people call you back if they want to speak with you; they delete your message if they don't. In fact, we've **never** been called back by an irate employer because of leaving him or her a voicemail message.

Effective Voicemail Messages

Of the many principles defining this program that contradict conventional job hunting teachings, voicemail is a major one. Conventional job hunting programs teach you to always push to get your contact on the telephone. That's because they believe an employer will rarely return "job hunter voicemails." Instead, they believe the employer will immediately delete such a message without giving it much thought. It's also taught that if leaving a voicemail is unavoidable, a job seeker must be as cryptic as possible, leaving enough of a "teaser" message to gain a call-back, but never letting on that they're looking for a job. Examples of "teaser" messages include *"I wanted to get your input on a project I'm working on," "I wanted to get your insight on the status of your industry,"* or other such "disguised" premises.

If you want to get a leader to think less of you when he/she calls you back, leave a voicemail message which disguises what you're really after. You're not fooling anyone – these people know what you're up to with such nuisance messages. If you want to impress someone, tell them straight up in your voicemail message what you are after, and how you can possibly add value to their organization. You will be taught how to do that later in this program.

It is absolutely true that most people will immediately delete voicemails, and usually within the first two seconds of hearing a message. They don't want to hear more time-wasting sales messages about the best credit rate, the latest wireless deal, or how a stranger is really going to save them lots of money. But, there is one important area where most **senior level** business people, 30/30's target market, actually listen to voicemails – **messages about talented people**. As mentioned earlier, successful leaders, like sports team coaches, are always keeping their eyes and ears open for the next star. If you can leave a voicemail which quickly grabs a leader's attention and describes how you can positively impact the organization, there is a good probability that leader will at least hit the "save" button or immediately call you back. Such a well-crafted and targeted message is a good example of putting our first major 30/30 principle into practice – Talent Intersecting Opportunity (see pages 8-9).

> *If used properly, voicemail is very successful in generating interviews.*

Neil spent more than 16 years leaving voicemails with company presidents, general managers, and business leaders. His messages described candidates for employment and openly sought interviews. He consistently received calls back, arranged interviews, and got those people hired. He also observed job hunters following his advice and leaving the voicemail messages themselves. They obtained interviews and job offers, and through all economic conditions

If you desire a quick and effective job search, then make voicemail your main strategy for contacting employers and uncovering opportunities.

Voicemail is much easier to use in a job search than people might believe, and job hunters who use it properly are very successful at generating interviews. However, you do not need to use voicemail for success with this program.

Despite all the positives of voicemail, things must be done correctly for success.

Voicemail is a "numbers game." Most who fail at generating interviews through voicemail fail because they simply did not leave a sufficient number of messages. For most campaigns, you must leave between 70 and 100 voicemails to generate between six and eight interviews – enough interviews for success. However, a very diligent person is capable of depositing that many voicemail messages in just **one day**, and someone who is serious about finding a job could easily leave that many messages over four days.

You also must pay close attention to **what** you say in your messages, **who** you leave your messages with, and **how** the messages are deposited.

Some reading this will still be nervous about telephoning a company. This tip should calm their fears: one of the best characteristics of this program is that you can experience success by leaving voicemail messages **after hours**, when there is no one at the offices you are targeting. That way, you will never speak with anyone who doesn't wish to speak with you because they must call you back. However, if you use voicemail after hours, you must increase the number of companies you contact because some companies do not have voicemail systems which operate after hours.

Voicemail is a good way to uncover opportunities and get interviews, but only if you leave several messages, and the messages are interesting enough to warrant a positive response. That presents an advantage for a job hunter because in a direct person-to-person telephone conversation, some people will immediately start thinking of ways to politely hand you off rather than listen to what you are saying. With voicemail, most will listen to your message carefully and then decide what to do. Some, roughly eight to ten percent, will actually call you back and do a telephone interview with you, which can lead to a face-to-face meeting and then a job offer.

The figure on page 24 illustrates how a voicemail message can result in interviews and job offers. In this figure, the candidate initiates the hiring process by leaving a compelling voicemail message with a key company contact – the person who has the power to hire, which will not be someone in human resources. That contact, in turn, requests a copy of the candidate's resume, which is then sent by email. After reviewing the resume, the contact invites the candidate to an initial job interview. This may be the first of several interviews with the company. If all goes well, the company will extend a job offer and then proceed to negotiate a compensation package.

When conducted within a structured 30/30 Placement Program, this process involves the intervention of a third party – a placement professional – who arranges the initial interview by voicemail. In this case, the placement professional coaches the candidate, conducts follow-up activities, and receives a commission for any placement.

To be effective with voicemail, you must learn the procedures for having your voicemail messages actually heard by your targeted decision-maker rather than have them screened and deleted by support staff. Before we learn voicemail procedures, let's discuss briefly electronic mail.

The Voicemail/Email Interview and Hiring Process

Electronic Mail (Email): The Second Best Job Hunting Tool Ever

Email is a key communication tool in our 30/30 program. However, for best results, email should be used only **after** establishing initial telephone or face-to-face contact. Nonetheless, email can be used as a means for making initial job search contact with leaders, and is very effective if used properly.

Corporate web pages frequently list a company's senior leaders and their email addresses. While they encourage people to email these executives, most executives will never see the emails because web-page email addresses are more for public relations purposes than actual communication; many executives receive thousands of emails. Some executives will actually email you back from their web-page email addresses, so we will use those addresses for this program. However, most leaders maintain one or two additional email addresses which they always use, and we need to acquire those addresses also.

Effectively emailing leaders requires obtaining the email addresses they actually use. There are two best ways to accomplish that. The first method is more difficult, but more effective. That is to call the company switchboard and ask directly for the email address of the person you are trying to reach. Simply say:

"My name is (your first and last name) and I am emailing (first and last name of the business leader...DO NOT say "Mr." or "Ms.") some information and need his/her email address."

Whatever email address you are given, respond with:

"No, not that one...I need his OTHER address."

She will give you another address, tell you she does not know of any other address, or say she does not have the authority to give it out. Thank her, hang up, and then proceed with the following second method for obtaining email addresses:

The second method requires a few minutes of research. You must first obtain the email format for the company. This is easily accomplished by going to the company's web page and exploring the various pages. Within the "Contact" page you should find at least one email address, such as info@XYZCompany.com. If not, then go to the company's "About Us" or "Home" pages and look for links with the names of anyone who works at the company. You should find at least one email address for someone at the company. If not, then "google" the company's name and somewhere in all the links that come up will be an email address for someone at that company. Use the format displayed with the name of the leader you want, but include addresses with variations.

Take, for example, a business named XYZ Company. The company's human resources manager's email address is Susan.Smith@XYZCompany.com. The company's president is John Jones. For emailing John Jones, you should try the addresses: John.Jones@ XYZ Company.com; John.Jones1@XYZCompany.com; John.Jones2@XYZCompany. com; and John.Jones3@XYZCompany.com. The odds are good that at least one or two of the three addresses is the "real" address for John Jones, president of XYZ Company, and he will receive your email. The other addresses will be returned as "non-deliverable" or, if there is another John Jones at the company, he will forward your email to Jones the president, or simply delete it.

Needless to say, when speaking with leaders, **always** ask for their email addresses. Almost all leaders will give their address to you, but only if you ask for it, **so do not fail to ask**. Email will become your primary means of communication with companies and their leaders after an initial interview is arranged.

Finally, never abuse the email privilege by sending a leader the same email more than twice, and **never** release email addresses to others without permission.

Voicemail Procedures

Voicemail facilitates communication with key decision-makers and it allows them to respond, or not respond, at their own discretion. As such, voicemail is essentially a non-confrontational form of communication. It provides a "softer" approach where your message is actually heard without interruption. However, that is only if the voicemail is left correctly.

As with email systems, most decision-makers usually have two voicemail boxes: one public, one "confidential" for real communication. Obviously, you want to access the confidential mailboxes.

Secretaries and office assistants listen to, screen, forward to others, or erase most of the messages in their boss's public mailbox. A voicemail from a job seeker will probably be erased or forwarded to Human Resources – the last place you want it to go. That is why you need the confidential mailboxes. Sometimes secretaries screen their boss's confidential mailbox, but that is not commonly done. Many business leaders listen alone to the messages in their confidential voicemail.

The following pages present the best procedures for getting your voicemail messages into confidential boxes and actually heard by the people who have the power to hire.

Accessing "Confidential" Voicemail Boxes

Phase II (Action) of 30/30 is when you will leave voicemail messages. Before leaving voicemails, however, your research from Phase I (Research and Planning) will result in your 30/30 Contact List containing the names of the companies and their leaders whose confidential voicemail boxes you desire to access. Here is the procedure for accessing the mailboxes:

1. **Dial the company's main switchboard.** You will encounter either a switchboard operator or voicemail menu. After hours, you should only encounter the voicemail menu.

   A. If you know the executive's name, and you encounter an assistant/switchboard operator, say these exact words clearly and **SLOWLY**:

      "Hi, this is (your FIRST and LAST name). (FIRST and LAST name)'s voicemail, please. Thanks."

      The operator will not question you because you asked for voicemail, not the person himself/herself. Also, it is unlikely that the business leader will pick up his/her telephone because most switchb   rd operators have a "voicemail only" extension option for a company's key people.

   B. If you do not know the name of the business leader, say these exact words **CLEARLY** and **SLOWLY:**

      "Hi, this is (your FIRST and LAST name). Who is the (title of the person in charge of the department you are seeking, such as "Director of Engineering")?"

      The slow, steady pace of your voice combined with the clear pronunciation of your name will cause the assistant/switchboard operator to assume you are a person of importance. Do not talk fast or forcefully, or you will trigger screening questions.

      She or he will name the person, and you should respond:

      "Please put me through to (use the person's FIRST NAME ONLY, do NOT say "Mr." or "Ms.") voicemail. Thanks."

As mentioned earlier, when asking for a leader's voicemail, not the person, you will be rarely questioned by operators or screeners. However, in the unlikely event you are questioned, you should politely ignore the question and respond:

> *"This is (your first and last name...SLOWLY!). I need (first name)'s voicemail. Put me through. Thanks."*

Do not answer her questions! With this method, you will be put through (if not, thank the person, hang up, and leave the voicemail after hours) because screeners know that **important people (such as key customers or senior executives) ignore screening questions, and keep repeating their names, waiting for recognition.** They do exactly what you just did, repeating their names slowly and clearly, and asking for the business leader's voicemail by using the leader's **first name**. The first name usage reinforces your importance, and most assistants will play it safe and put you through because they plan on listening to your voicemail anyway. What they don't realize is that you will deposit your message in the leader's confidential voicemail box and avoid their screening.

C. If you get the voicemail menu instead of an assistant, be patient and listen to all the options before making any selections. Wait for the "Spell by Name" option. You should know the person's name from your research in Phase I of the campaign. Then proceed to #2.

2. **Spell the name of the person by using the telephone keypad as indicated in the menu.** You should get that person's main voicemail box. If you hear "name not recognized" instead, you should hit the pound (#) or star (*) key, one of which should give you the operator. Revert to the procedure you learned for obtaining a name from an operator/assistant. If it is after hours, move to the next company on your Contact List.

3. **At the tone, read the message you've prepared about yourself**, which you developed in Phase I.

4. **When you are done reading your message, hit the pound (#) button, *even if not prompted to do so*.** With most voicemail systems, that will give you a message saying "Message Delivery Options." If not, there will be silence, or a voice saying "incorrect selection" or "message stopped."

If there is silence, or a voice saying "message stopped," hang up. There is no private delivery option. The message will be delivered. If the voice says "incorrect selection, please try again," hit the star (*) key. This should get you to "Message Delivery Options." If not, hang up. Your message will be delivered.

5. **Once in "Message Delivery Options," wait patiently through all the options and the long, painful pauses between each option.** These pauses are

long because they're designed to trip up telemarketers into making a selection that will keep them out of the private mailboxes. In most systems, the options voice usually says something like this:

> *"To deliver your message 'now' or with 'regular delivery,' hit the pound (#) key."* If you do not hit the pound key, a long pause will follow, then . . .

> *"For 'urgent' delivery, hit the star (*) key."* Here's where the system hopes to trick you. "Urgent" delivery is what (unsuccessful) salespeople will usually select, assuming the message will receive the prospect's immediate attention. In most systems, the message actually **does** get immediate attention . . . by an office staffer who screens and deletes the message!

After the "urgent delivery" option, there will be another long pause . . . then:

> *"To mark this message 'private' or 'confidential,' hit (a key)."* Hit the key. This is where you want to leave your message. After leaving the message, log the message as "sent" in your Contact List.

Voicemail Follow-Up

If you do not hear back from this person within two days, leave the exact same voicemail again. Do not leave a voicemail with the same person three times, but **always make two attempts** if there is no response. Neil has arranged many interviews over the years where it took two voicemails to get a call-back from a leader. Had he not left a second voicemail, he would not have been able to arrange the interviews.

Some systems will have additional options such as the ability to review your message and record it again. If you feel you "blew" your message, go ahead and re-record it, but be sure to repeat the procedures for leaving it in the private mailbox.

For companies with a switchboard number ending in "00," and if you have difficulty obtaining the names of key leaders there, dial the main switchboard and add the suffixes "01," "02," "03" on up until a human being picks up the telephone. (Example: if the company's number is 123-456-7000, try dialing 123-456-7001; 7002; 7003; etc.). Simply say *"I'm sorry, I think I've got the wrong extension. Who is the (title of the leader you want)?"* The person who answered will usually tell you without hesitation.

Some people may feel uncomfortable leaving voicemail messages in a person's "private" or "confidential" mailbox. Don't be one of those people. After all, if the recipient is not interested, he or she will instantly delete the message, won't even attempt to remember your name, and that will be the end of it. In all the years Neil has been using these techniques, he has **never** received an angry call-back for leaving a message in a private voicemail box!

The Internet, 30/30, and the Art of "Candidate Contrived Coincidence"

Most job hunting books and experts emphasize the Internet as a great tool for uncovering opportunities. It is, but not in the way that is taught or advocated. You must be careful in how you handle online application instructions. Ironically, if you follow the online instructions on how to submit your application, chances are you won't get results from your efforts. Also, the Internet is a great networking tool, especially if you use such websites as LinkedIn.

Using the Internet

The Internet is very important to your success, but mostly as an **informational tool**. At the same time, it can be a double-edged sword for many job seekers. After all, it's used by employers to research candidates – learn more about them by examining their online presence. If, for example, you are a member of a social or business networking site, such as Facebook and LinkedIn, or have a web page, the Internet can hurt your employment prospects. Make certain that everything about you on these sites is professional. Remove anything which can be interpreted as negative, such as photos of you dressed provocatively, drinking, smoking,

> *Check out your online presence to make sure you present a very professional image to prospective employers.*

tattoos showing, partying, or quotes with any hint of profanity or "edginess." Smart employers check out these sites as part of their screening process. A professional online presence will add value to you as a job candidate; an unprofessional presence will hurt you.

Take, for example, your own online presence. When was the last time you "Googled" your name? Are you regularly monitoring your Internet presence by entering your name into Google Alerts (www.google.com/alerts) – a critical action ALL job seekers should take for finding out what others are posting about them on the Internet? As an ex-offender, whether misdemeanor or felony conviction, your arrests, adjudication, and criminal record might be documented on the Internet – something you need to be prepared to deal with throughout your job search. In today's wired world, there's no place to hide or lie!

For job seekers, the Internet's real value is found in **researching companies, job openings, and people as well as sending emails**, but never as a good tool for actually acquiring interviews. Even though they represent real openings, online job advertisements should be approached as job "leads" only. Use these "leads" to obtain interviews by **circumventing** the conventional hiring process. You need a way to bypass the thousands of online applicants who answer online job postings. Many of these candidates would be ideal matches for the positions, but, sadly for them (and good for you), these candidates will not receive an interview **because** they did exactly as directed in the advertisements.

The Secrets of "Candidate Contrived Coincidence"

The unconventional method for bypassing online applicants and putting yourself at the head of the Internet interviewing line is what Neil calls the **"Candidate Contrived Coincidence" technique**.

You should use the Internet for researching Internet job boards, corporate web pages, newspapers, and publications with job advertisements (or "job postings") for positions which interest you, and which you are capable of performing. Each ad should be for a position located within your targeted geographic location, or **Search Zone** (SZ). Print out the ads and keep copies of them in a folder.

Read and study each ad carefully. Your goal is to clearly understand each position and to identify the company **location** with the opening. The location is usually revealed within the ad itself, or you can figure it out from clues in the ad. However, you must be careful because many online ads are run from a company's headquarters for positions located far away from your targeted location. You also want two names: the name of the senior manager at the site, and the name of the department manager with the actual opening. Ignore the name mentioned in the advertisement. That's a Human Resources person.

> *The key to Candidate Contrived Coincidence is to do what others are not doing, such as make a call when an ad says "no phone calls."*

The best way to obtain key names is through your software, by researching the company's web page, or from its online Chamber of Commerce listing. If you are skilled enough, you can also simply call the switchboard and use the techniques you learned earlier. Also, don't worry if an ad says "No phone calls accepted." You won't be calling Human Resources, the people who wrote the ad and do not want telephone calls. Also, remember, the key to Candidate Contrived Coincidence is to do what others are not doing. If an ad says "no phone calls," that means the majority of responders are not going to call, and those who call will have a higher probability of getting through to the person with the opening. Finally, never inform a switchboard that you are calling about an advertised position, since they will pass your call immediately to Human Resources.

Contact Those With the Power to Hire

You need to identify the person the position reports to because that is the person who **feels the urgency** of the opening, and also the person who will make the final hiring decision. Hiring decisions are not made by Human Resources people; they are made by the person a position reports to. To find out who a position reports to requires knowledge of the different functional areas within an organization. That is not difficult. For example, if an advertised position is for a **manufacturing project engineer** or **process engineer**, the job most likely reports to a **Manager of Engineering**. If the position is for a **production supervisor**, then it reports to a **Production Manager**. If an advertisement is for a **sales representative** for a territory or city, the position will report to a **District Sales Manager**. If it is for a **warehouse supervisor**, it will report to a **Distribution Center Manager** or **Warehouse Manager**.

If you have a career going in a certain field, you will know the titles of the people to ask for within your field. However, as a rule of thumb, in most companies, **supervisors**, **representatives**, and **engineers** report to **managers**; **managers** report to **directors**; **directors** report to **presidents** and **general managers**.

Candidate Contrived Coincidence

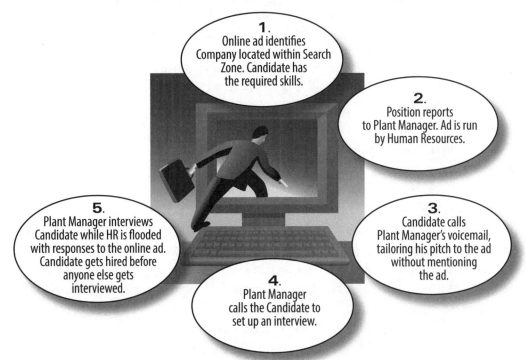

1. Online ad identifies Company located within Search Zone. Candidate has the required skills.

2. Position reports to Plant Manager. Ad is run by Human Resources.

3. Candidate calls Plant Manager's voicemail, tailoring his pitch to the ad without mentioning the ad.

4. Plant Manager calls the Candidate to set up an interview.

5. Plant Manager interviews Candidate while HR is flooded with responses to the online ad. Candidate gets hired before anyone else gets interviewed.

The above figure illustrates the interactive dynamics of Candidate Contrived Coincidence when used by a 30/30 Placement Program Campaign Manager (CM) to gain an interview for a Campaign Candidate (CC) for an advertised position. As a candidate, you can do this on your own without the assistance of a third party professional.

One additional rule of thumb worth remembering when responding to online ads: If an advertised position is at a company site with over 1,000 employees, then obtain only the name of the department manager with the opening. The top leader at the site will most likely not respond to your message or, worse, kill it by passing your message to Human Resources.

Script Your Voicemail Messages and Letters

Once you have the names, you are now ready to write voicemail presentations for each advertisement. Each presentation should be **tailored** exactly to each advertisement. You will also send tailored letters and email messages if voicemail does not succeed in gaining a response, or if the very idea of leaving voicemail messages seems too stressful for you.

Your goal is to leave a voicemail message with both the senior leader on site, and the department manager with the opening. In leaving the messages, do so using the exact voicemail procedures you learned earlier. Each voicemail message should be tailored to each advertisement and should emphasize your skills and experience as they apply directly to each position, but **do not mention anything about an advertisement in your message!!!** Your message should sound something like this):

> "Mr. /Ms. (Manager's name), my name is (your name) and I'm a certified electrician experienced in working with large commercial projects (briefly tailor your description to whatever the ad says they want, but do not misrepresent your experience). I'm living in (your location) but moving to your area soon. I will be visiting for house hunting and was wondering if I could send you my resume or actually meet with you for a few minutes while I'm in town. I don't know if you have any current or potential needs right now, but if you do, I'd love to meet you to discuss them. Again, my name is (your name) and my number is (your number). Thanks!"

If you happen to live near where the advertised position is located, say *"I live in the area so there is no relocation expense with me . . . and I am setting aside (dates) for meetings and would enjoy meeting with you."*

Note the **precise** words of this message. What you did **not** say is as important as what you did say. First, you did not mention the ad or use the word "interviews" in your presentation. (Had you done so, your voicemail would be passed to Human Resources.) Second, you did not say anything that is untrue because even though there was an advertised position, you do not know for certain if the advertisement accurately describes the needs of the organization. Third, you tailored your experience to the advertisement, to the closest extent truthfully possible. Finally, you stated your location, a place distant to the company, but that you are moving to their location soon, will be visiting, and both of which mean no relocation or interview travel expenses for the company.

If this is done properly, many managers will assume it is purely coincidental that someone who can fill his or her department's present needs **drops in out of nowhere** from a distant location. It is that **coincidence**, combined with a tight window for a visit with no travel cost to the company, which causes a manager to respond quickly. Be prepared for a returned call sounding something like this:

> "(Your name), this is (name) and I am the (department) manager at XYZ Company. A few days ago, you left a voicemail with me. *It just so happens* that we are looking for someone right now. I would be very interested in speaking with you."

Not surprisingly, when you use this Candidate Contrived Coincidence approach, you'll have a high probability of moving ahead of thousands of online applicants whose resumes will be stuck in the Human Resources department, will never be seen, and who will never be interviewed.

When you return this manager's call, your goal will be to arrange an interview for yourself. You will be taught how to do that in the section "Setting Up Appointments From Voicemail Call-Backs." If you do not receive a call-back from a voicemail message within two days, then leave the same voicemail message a second time with this same manager. If there is no response within two days with this second attempt, then move to your second method of contact: email.

Your last method of contact shall be a personal letter to the person the position reports to, but you will send it to his/her **home address**, not the company. We will cover email messages and letters in detail later.

Always Use a High-Touch Versus a High-Tech Approach

Candidate Contrived Coincidence is highly effective. It is amazing (and amusing) how often a manager with an opening hires someone who comes to his attention from this approach, even prior to considering **anyone** who answered the company's online advertisement. With online advertisements, hundreds of fully qualified applicants apply for positions, yet rarely does someone actually get hired from the pool of candidates who apply. **The person who gets hired is the one who bypasses all the other applicants.**

Technology is a valuable tool for job hunters, but those who use "high-tech" as a substitute for a "high-touch" technique, such as Candidate Contrived Coincidence, will lose almost every time.

Mail (Post), 30/30, and Home-Targeted Letters

The postal system has always played a major role in job hunting. For decades, the mail has been the primary means used by job hunters for contacting business leaders. A well written cover letter combined with a resume tailored to a specific position, mailed to a company, actually does get positive results . . . about once every 40 letters. That means a job hunter needs to "mass mail" around 240 letters if he/she desires to obtain between four and six interviews. A more effective approach is needed.

Back in 1986, a hand-addressed envelope arrived at Neil's home one day. The postmark was from the area where Neil went to college. There was no name above the return address, just an address. Neil opened the envelope, finding a resume with a cover letter. The writer, a college friend he had not heard from since graduation, wrote that he had heard that Neil was in the "job hunting business" and was curious if Neil knew anyone who might be interested in someone with his background. He also apologized for sending his resume to Neil's home, explaining that he did not know the name of Neil's company and that he had looked up his address in the telephone directory.

The most effective way to mail resumes and cover letters is to send them to the homes of the people you want to reach.

The old college friend, either by accident or by his clever design, opened Neil's eyes to one of the most effective ways to contact leaders. Mail is mostly ineffective in job hunting, because it rarely even reaches the leader for which it is intended. The mail is opened by secretaries and screeners, and a job hunter's letter will be filed, thrown away, or given to Human Resources, which is the same as being thrown away in many companies! However, people actually read letters that are sent to their homes, even the busiest executives. And, unbelievably, 85% (or more) of all business and community leaders are listed in the telephone directory, along with their home addresses, and this applies to even the most influential people.

The most effective way to mail resumes and cover letters is to send them to the **homes** of the people you want to reach. Handwrite the business leader's name and address on the envelope, and also handwrite your name and return address on it so the recipient realizes it is a real letter from a real person, not junk mail or a form letter. Enclose your typed resume accompanied by a cover letter which says something similar to what appears in the example below. Only a very unpleasant (and odd) person would not be impressed by such creativity. You may not receive a call right away, but you can be sure the reader will at least save your letter in his own personal files rather than throw it away or pass it off to someone without instructing that person to contact you for an interview.

This technique is very effective for almost anyone who has a marketable skill. The key is the letter sets you apart from just about anyone that leader has ever heard from. The letter should also be tailored to the individual and his/her company, and should be flattering, but not overdone. You should also send only a small number of these letters (perhaps 15) because you don't want your letters flooding the marketplace and diminishing their personal touch. Pick the leaders you most want to impress and write them. Finally, you might ask how you know you are writing the right person if there is more than one person in the telephone directory with the same name as the business leader you desire to reach. You don't. However, send a letter to each person with that name and the chances are the right one should receive it. The others will simply shrug their shoulders and think *"He has the wrong one...but this is a pretty smart person!"*

Dear Mr. /Ms. (Name);

My name is (your name) and I am writing you because I have learned that you are the president of (name of company), a company I have great interest in.

I hope you do not mind my writing you at your home. I am doing so for two reasons: First, I know you will probably actually read this if it is sent to your home and it will not be screened out by your able assistant and, second, you will realize right away that I am a creative and resourceful person who will take reasonable risks to achieve worthy objectives.

I'm a certified electrician specializing in major commercial projects. While I have worked as an independent contractor, I've decided to pursue a full-time position with a major construction firm with the stature and reputation such as yours. I have had some great experiences for a young person and would love to spend a few minutes meeting with you to tell you about them, as well as show you what I can bring to your team. I don't know if you have any present or potential needs right now, but I am versatile and believe I can add value in many areas. I am visiting your area for job hunting the week of (dates) and would be honored to meet you or one of your company's managers at any time which is convenient for you.

I hope to hear from you soon.

Sincerely and respectfully,

(Your first and last name)

4

Research and Planning

"Research and planning play critical roles in quickly organizing and implementing an effective 30/30 job search. You should focus on developing powerful Contact Lists and savvy Telephone Scripts that motivate employers to interview and hire you."

THE OBJECTIVE OF PHASE I is to construct a complete **Campaign Plan**, and to do so within the first three or four days. The Campaign Plan consists of five elements:

1. Contact List
2. Advertisements and opportunity leads
3. Pre-written scripts (voicemail presentations, setting up appointments, answers to employer responses)
4. Basic resumes and tailored resumes
5. Email scripts

The Campaign Plan is the "battle plan" you will execute during Phase II. Let's examine each of these five components in the Campaign Plan and identify how to make each element work for you.

Develop and Target a Contact List

A Contact List includes a list of companies you will target and the leaders who work for those companies. Even though this is a Contact List, that does not mean you will call anyone at this initial stage of your job search. Calling is what job placement consultants do when they implement 30/30 for clients.

The fastest way to develop a contact list is to access the Internet via a computer. If you're still locked up behind a firewall, obviously the step-by-step "digital communication in the free world" instructions in this chapter may be somewhat frustrating. Nonetheless, bear with us as we share useful strategies that will become very important once you re-enter the free world and thus have access to the digital world.

While we recommended using the free website Manta (www.manta.com) in Chapter 3, the more powerful, and costly, websites for identifying both companies and their competitors are PowerFinder (www.infousa.com) and SalesGenie (www.salesgenie. com), which we make reference to in this chapter for outlining the contact list building process. If you don't have access to the Internet, all is not lost. Later in this chapter we outline a powerful computer- and Internet-free approach (drive-by, walk-in, paper directory) for building your contact list (see pages 44-46).

Assuming you are targeting businesses, each company entered on the Contact List should include the telephone number, name of the town where located, name of the senior manager, sales volume, number of employees, and distance in miles from your ideal geographic point, or center of your Search Zone. You should also look quickly through each company's website and make brief notes regarding products, services, and latest press releases. If you do not know a web address, simply do a Google search of the company's name, and the company's web address should come up. Until you obtain an interview or a meeting with someone from a company, you should not go further than this level of basic research. At this point, it is not an efficient use of your time to perform in-depth research. You should spend only a few minutes researching each company for inclusion on your Contact List.

For best results, you should compile a Contact List of 75 to 150 companies. You will also list the key leaders at those companies, and that list can become lengthy. The more leaders you identify, the greater the number of contacts you can make, and the better your chances of getting interviews.

On the surface, listing 75 to 150 companies may seem challenging. It isn't, but that's only if you are willing to include smaller companies you have never heard of before and not focus solely upon the larger companies which everyone knows about. Some of the greatest opportunities, or what we call Zones of Opportunities (remember ZOOs from Chapter 2?), are found with smaller companies.

> *For best results, you should compile a Contact List of 75 to 150 companies, which should yield 4 to 6 job interviews*

With 150 companies on your Contact List, you should be able to obtain between four and six interviews for yourself, regardless of economic conditions. In fact, with that number, you might even generate up to as many as 10 or more interviews. You should always work very hard to list 150 companies for your Contact List, even though successful 30/30 campaigns can result from far fewer than that number. In fact, Neil has seen as few as 20 companies produce positive results, but those were within rural Search Zones which lacked companies in the area. Also, 20 companies can produce 60 or more leaders to contact.

Always strive to target as many companies as possible for your Contact List. Do not ignore smaller or privately owned companies, or companies which seem unimpressive. All can produce superb opportunities for you if you handle things correctly. The more companies you list, the more potential interviews. We will share with you later how to identify companies for your Contact List.

A Company's "Entry Points" (Manufacturing Plant)

Preferred Order of Contact:

1. General Manager or President

2. Production Manager

3. Maintenance Manager

4. Human Resources Manager

The majority of companies will have multiple contacts or "entry points" for you, as emphasized in the above illustration, for implementing your unconventional job search that will quickly outshine the competition. If, for example, a **company president** does not want to meet you, then contact the company's **general manager**. If the general manager is unreceptive, then contact the **department head** where you think your skills would fit. Neil has seen many times where the first two contacts at a company were not helpful, and the third contact arranged an interview.

Since key decision-makers within a company will most likely not talk to each other about you, don't mention that you contacted others at the company, or worry that one might be upset if he was unresponsive to meeting you and learns that his colleague in the next office met you. That's one reason why this program will work even in places where there are few companies.

The following discussion is an example of how to construct a Contact List using an Internet search engine plus PowerFinder or SalesGenie software. It can be adapted to other software programs and organizational schemes. The important point throughout this example is to compile a comprehensive set of contracts from which you can implement the first and subsequent stages of your 30/30 job search program.

Focus Your Search in a Specific Geographic Location

The software will instruct you on how to load it. It will begin by showing an alphabetical listing of every company and residence located within the geographic region the software is referencing, just as in the telephone book.

At the top of the screen, there will be a "Name" box. If your present address is the location where you want to continue living, type your name in the box using your last name, then first. If you will be relocating, type in the name of any person or business whose home/business is located in your Search Zone. Type in their last name first, then first name; or the name of the business. The software will produce a list of all the people or businesses with that name.

From the list, you will recognize either your name and address, or the specific person or business you are looking for. Their address will become the exact spot on the ground from which you will find employment within 30 miles, i.e., the center of your Search Zone. If you do not know any people or businesses in your Search Zone, then use the City Hall or Town Hall address. With the address you have selected, click on "Tools" on the taskbar. A menu will appear. From this menu, click on the "Set Geo Center Point Location" option and a box will appear. Click on the "Currently Selected" taskbar in the box, and then click on the "Set as Center" bar at the bottom of the box.

You have now set the exact center point of your Search Zone and are ready to identify the best 75-150 companies within your Search Zone for inclusion on your Contact List.

Identify Companies With Contact List Potential

Always begin your company searches by identifying the easiest companies to find, and those will be the companies with the best name recognition and/or major employers within your Search Zone. These will be large manufacturing plants, distribution centers, and headquarters groups. They are best found by using an Internet search engine and performing the following searches on the Internet:

> Search #1: *(Name of Town/City largest employers)*
> Search #2: *(Name of Town/City major employers)*
> Search #3: *(Name of Town/City manufacturers)*
> Search #4: *(Name of Town/City warehouses)*

For most locations within the United States, the searches listed above should yield a wide variety of companies and industries. Go to each company's website and find out the names, telephone numbers, and email addresses of each company's leaders. Add this information to your Contact List. Some programs, such as PowerFinder (www.infou sa.com) and SalesGenie (www.salesgenie.com), will allow you to identify company competitors. If a company's competitors are within your Search Zone, list them on your Contact List.

The next step in building your Contact List is to search for companies within your Search Zone which do the kinds of things you have done in your career or in the previous jobs you have held. For example, if you have banking experience, you should locate all the banks within your Search Zone. If you are an engineer, you should locate all the engineering firms and manufacturing plants. If you are a pharmaceutical sales representative, you should identify the companies which sell pharmaceuticals, and so on. The best way to do that is through an Internet search in combination with your software. Here is an example of the search format for four separate Internet searches:

Search #1: *(Your industry City/Town)*
Search #2: *(Your industry County)*
Search #3: *(Your industry State)*
Search #4: *(Similar to your industry City/Town)*

The following is an example of a real search that was conducted by a client using the Google search engine (www.google.com) for locating banks in or around Austintown, Ohio.

Enter into the search box: **Banks Austintown Ohio**

This search produces a list of more than 20 banks within or near this mid-size Ohio town. The list includes each bank's location, operating hours, website, and directions.

Using the listings produced from these searches, visit each company's website and find the names, telephone numbers, and email addresses of each company's leaders, and add the information to your Contact List. Next, type the company names into SalesGenie or PowerFinder and find their competitors. If a competitor has a presence within your Search Zone, add them to your Contact List, along with their leader's contact information.

At this point, it's important to emphasize keeping an open mind to a wide variety of companies, industries, and potential opportunities. Don't focus solely on your career field. That's because you are searching within a specific geographic location. Consider our banking example: if your career has been in banking, then you should try to locate all the banks within your Search Zone. However, the Google search will bring up a specific number of banks, such as the 10 listed on the Internet for Austintown, Ohio. Keep in mind that even though there were only some listed by Google on the Internet, there are probably more banks in and around Austintown and your job is to locate all of them. The first 10 banks can yield 20 or 30 leader contacts, but that is probably too low a number of contacts for a successful outcome for most 30/30 searches.

> ***Don't focus solely on companies in your career field. Broaden your search to include companies connected to them.***

Let's return to the banking example. Once you identify all the banks within your Search Zone, you should next identify all the companies with **any kind of connection** to banking and finance, such as financial services companies, credit unions, mortgage companies, and so forth. After these, you should identify companies which may have finance and accounting departments. You may be surprised by how many organizations employ people with banking and financial skills but are not banks.

After you have searched for companies within or related to your career field, move next to searching for consumer products companies (i.e., companies which produce and sell products people use every day such as toiletries, food and beverages). Most consumer products companies have a division, branch, warehouse, or sales office in every mid-size town across the United States and that's because their products need to be available everywhere and at all times. Consumer products companies tend to have high turnover of employees, mostly due to a very fast pace of operations. Many of these organizations operate around the clock manufacturing and shipping their products to sales outlets, and some employees at these companies feel overworked and leave.

Because of constant employee turnover, most consumer product companies always have vacant positions – a process that generates many Zones of Opportunity (ZOOs). Identifying consumer product company locations within your Search Zone can be tricky because these companies want people to contact their consumer information call centers, not their field locations. For that reason, you should ignore the telephone numbers on their product packaging or in the telephone book and, instead, obtain the information you need through the Internet and your software. To do that, look at your favorite household products and, using the manufacturer's name or the product brand name, do the following searches:

Search #1: *(Brand name City/Town)*
Search #2: *(Manufacturer's name City/Town)*

Here is an example:

Enter into the search engine box: *(Coca Cola Norfolk, Virginia)*

This search yields much information about Coca Cola's distribution facility in downtown Norfolk, Virginia. It also provides links to additional Coca Cola sites. To find out who the key leaders are at this facility, more research may be required (if you do not wish to simply call the facility and ask who the general manager is, using the techniques discussed earlier in this manual). The following search should yield information which includes the name of the general manager for this facility. However, you may need to read through several listings to learn who the person is:

Enter in the search box: *(Coca Cola Norfolk, Virginia general manager)*

As another example, and once again using Norfolk, Virginia as the geographic location, or Search Zone, the following search should yield information on Frito Lay's sales office(s) and/or warehouse(s) for serving the location:

Enter into the search box: *(Frito Lay Norfolk, Virginia)*

Within the first three listings resulting from this search are the location, telephone number, and general manager's name for Frito Lay's warehouse and sales center serving Norfolk, Virginia. This information should be added to your Contact List.

The brand names and types of consumer products are almost limitless. A walk through a grocery store will give you great ideas about companies to add to your Contact List. That's because every product you see in the store arrived at the store by truck; the truck was loaded at what is most likely a local warehouse, and each truck was loaded with the types and amounts of products as determined by a salesperson from a local sales office. Additionally, as a general rule of thumb, the more perishable the product, such as ice cream and dairy products, the closer to the store will be the manufacturing plant, sales offices, and warehouses for producing, selling, and shipping the product. That means many of these products will come from sites within your Search Zone.

Although many of the consumer products you see in a store will be sold and shipped through company-owned sales offices and warehouses, just as many may be sold and shipped through private distributors who are licensed by the consumer product company to sell their products. Distributors of consumer products face the same employee turnover issues as the consumer products companies themselves because they sell and ship the same products and have the same fast pace of operations. Accordingly, distributors have ongoing opportunities (ZOOs), so all the consumer product distributors in your Search Zone should also be added to your Contact List.

If you have skills that seem to have nothing to do with consumer products, such as skills in maintenance and repair of equipment, do not think that consumer products companies cannot use your skills. All buildings, and all the equipment within them, require maintenance, whether it is a warehouse, sales office, or retail store. The maintenance is performed either by a maintenance professional who is employed by the organization, or by an external maintenance contractor. Either way, there are people who work in the buildings doing what you can do. Include the companies on your Contact List.

At this point, you can see how your Contact List is beginning to take shape. Thus far, it should consist of the (1) companies and their leaders within your Search Zone which are the major employers within your Search Zone, (2) companies from your career field, (3) companies which use similar skills from your career field, (4) consumer products companies and their licensed distributors, and (5) the competitors of all of the above. Since each company on your Contact List has at least one (and probably two or three) business leader who can be contacted, your list of names of business leaders is growing. Every business leader has Zones of Opportunity for their organization or area of responsibility within their organization. As your Contact List expands, you should begin to feel increasingly confident that wherever your Search Zone is, there are many people who can hire you, or who can at least lead you to the people who can hire you.

Even so, we will expand your Contact List even further and add more companies and business leaders to it.

Three Ways to Expand Your Contact List

There are three simple methods for adding many more companies to your Contact List. The first and easiest method is to identify the organizations that are located **physically near the companies** you already listed on your Contact List. We already know these "neighboring" organizations are within the Search Zone.

Most manufacturing plants, warehouses, and distribution centers are located in **industrial parks** or areas zoned for such businesses, and most business software will identify the industrial parks. Using Manta, PowerFinder, or SalesGenie, type into the "Name" data field each manufacturing plant, warehouse, and distribution company you have listed on your Contact List. After typing a company name, click on the "address" taskbar. A list of the organizations located on the same street will be produced. Visit the websites of each of these organizations and add to your Contact List the ones which seem interesting. Then, as before, use your software to identify the competitors of each of these organizations and determine whether or not they are within your Search Zone. If so, add them to your Contact List also.

After identifying the companies within industrial parks, perform this exact same procedure for **office parks**. Using the office addresses of companies already on your Contact List, you can identify each company's neighbors in the office park – and even in the **same building**. A large office park can yield literally dozens of companies and business leaders for your Contact List. In fact, Neil has seen job hunters limit their job search to one specific office park and succeed in finding satisfying employment there.

A second method for expanding your Contact List is by using **online satellite mapping** sites such as Google Maps (maps.google.com). A Search Zone contains significant geographic territory, encompassing 60 miles east to west and 60 miles north to south (30 mile radius to the center of your Search Zone). Using satellite views of your Search Zone, "zoom in" on places with large buildings clustered together. Often, these are industrial areas or office parks (large buildings standing alone tend to be residential apartments, condos, etc.). Next, write down the names of the roads and streets where these buildings are located. Type these roads and street names into the search engine or "Google" them, and a list of what is located on them should be produced. For businesses, screen each organization and add to your Contact List those which appeal to you. Next, type the name of each road and street into other search engines and find out what is located on them, such as sites containing commercial real estate assessments and tax records.

A third and final simple method for expanding your Contact List is to visit the **Chamber of Commerce** websites for each city or town within your Search Zone. Start by visiting this gateway Chamber website: www.chamberofcommerce.com. Click on "Resource Directory," then on "Local Chambers of Commerce"; enter the name of the town(s) you are checking out. Then click on the Chamber website of that town. Check out the business categories listed on the site for those areas of interest to you. Most of these local sites identify member companies by industry and function. Most of these sites also list the names and contact information for each company's senior managers. Once you have this information, screen each company and add to your Contact List those which interest you. The figure on page 43 shows an example of a completed Contact List.

If after screening using the above methods you do not have at least 75-85 companies listed in your Contact List, you should now add small companies to your plan, the "mom and pops," the companies which you would not expect to have many opportunities for job seekers. Small companies are those with less than $5 million in sales volume, and even though they are small, they can be **very** worthwhile to pursue. For one thing, the owners are usually close by, and therefore you have easier access to the person who has the true vision for the company and is the ultimate decision-maker on hiring. Additionally, small companies can lead to big opportunities. For example, an owner might be looking for a successor to actually own his successful business.

Example of a Complete Contact/Call Plan

Company Name	Telephone Number	Town/ Location	Sales Volume	Number of Employees	Senior Manager	Distance from Search Center
ABC Manufacturing	123-456-1212	Jacksontown	20-30m	150	Bill Smith	10 miles west
DEF Wholesale	123-456-1212	Jacksontown	10-15	40	Ray Jones	4 miles south
HIJ Mechanical	123-456-1212	Smithtown	20m	60	Howard Jones	19 miles west
Additional Companies	Additional Phone #s	Additional Towns	Additional Sales	Additional Employees	Additional Managers	Additional Distances

250-300 Total Companies Listed

It should also be noted that many retailers, convenience stores, and fast food chains such as Target, Walmarts, Southland Corporation (7-Eleven), and Wendy's should not be ignored because of the pre-conceived notion that such stores will only put you behind a sales counter earning a minimum wage. These companies have superb opportunities, especially in their district management offices and regional warehouses. To locate the district offices and regional warehouses, call any of their retail stores located within your Search Zone. Ask for the telephone number of the local district office or local warehouse. If he or she does not know the number, get it from the manager on duty. Once you have the number, you can type it into any Internet search engine or key websites (try, for example, www.switchboard.com or www.411.com) and the address of the office or warehouse will come up. You can also do this by using PowerFinder or SalesGenie. Click on the "Phone" taskbar and type in the telephone number you received, including area code. The local district office or regional warehouse will come up on the screen. Click on the "More Info" box in the upper right-hand corner. This will give you the complete data file which includes the name of the District Manager or Distribution Center (warehouse) Manager.

Completed Contact List Characteristics

Based upon our experience, a Contact List for a mid-size (150,000 population) geographic area will usually consist of the following numbers and sizes of companies:

- 5-10 very large companies. (Fortune 500 manufacturing plants, distribution centers, and large private companies of 500 or more employees and over $100 million in annual sales volume, i.e., the "major employers" of the Search Zone.)

- 10-20 large companies. (Companies with up to 250 employees and $20-50 million in annual sales volume.)

- 20-40 mid-size companies. (Companies with up to 100 employees and $10-20 million in annual sales volume.)

- 40-50 small companies. (Companies with fewer than 20 employees and less than $5 million in annual sales volume.)

Depending upon the geography of your Search Zone, the number, size, industry type, and distance from the center of your Search Zone will vary for Contact List companies. For example, an engineer using this program in a remote part of Maine required a Search Zone which extended out to 40 miles from his home in order to identify 126 companies for his Contact List. Due mostly to Maine's geography and demographics, his Contact List consisted primarily of small and mid-size companies, and it had only **one** "very large" company, a nationally known shipyard.

This person was hired on the **37th** day of his campaign by a mid-size manufacturer located about 40 miles from his home. The distance was not a problem for him because long commutes are common in Maine.

Conversely, a transitioning military person using this program used his in-laws' home located in the suburbs of a major industrial city in Ohio as the center of his Search Zone. His Contact List consisted of over **200** companies, most of which were large or very large, and **all** of the companies were located within just **20 miles** from his in-laws' home. He was hired by a large company located only **eight miles** from their home.

Worth noting is that the greatest number of opportunities for you will come from companies within the mid-size category, companies which have $10-$20 million in annual sales volume and fewer than 100 employees, or are $10-$20 million divisions of larger companies located within the Search Zone. This is where you will find the most ZOOs and company owners and managers who are willing to take **action** on them by **creating** positions for outstanding people who can solve problems, add value, help the company grow, or fulfill the owner's vision for the future of the company. Accordingly, it is strongly recommended that you plan on contacting **all** the mid-size companies in your Search Zone, regardless of the industries they are in.

Additional Contact List Resources

It is easy to see how difficult it would be to construct a Contact List within four days without using a computer. Nonetheless, it can be done, but doing so requires resource materials for identifying companies by location, telephone number, products, services, annual sales volume, and key leadership. In constructing your Contact List without a computer, use the resource materials noted in the following paragraphs.

Finding companies can be accomplished through low-tech means. In fact, one of the most effective low-tech methods for adding companies to a Contact List is to get in your car and simply **drive around your Search Zone**, writing down the names of companies that appear interesting. Also, **walking into the lobbies** of office buildings and writing down the names of companies leasing office space can be very productive.

The best "paper" resources, which can be found at many public libraries, are Chamber of Commerce Membership Directories, State Manufacturers' Directories, and Business-to-Business Yellow Pages. There are many other resource publications, but these are the most productive. It is important to re-emphasize here that your Contact List should not involve any deep research about a company until after you have an interview scheduled with them. At this point, you simply need enough information to make an effective approach to the companies.

The Chambers of Commerce throughout the United States publish membership directories. These directories are the paper copies of the online directories and are very useful. You can find them in the reference section of your local public library. They can be purchased simply by contacting the Chamber of Commerce for your Search Zone. In fact, if your Search Zone is a major metropolitan area, the Chamber of Commerce Membership Directory may be the **best** resource for a very complete and effective Contact List. These directories have detailed information on member companies and include the names and often the direct-dial telephone numbers and "real" email addresses to the key leaders at the member firms.

Each state's commerce department publishes a State Manufacturers Directory, which should be available in your local library. These directories include every manufacturer in the state and categorize them by location, products, industries, and size. The information provided is more than sufficient for your Contact List screening. The best way to use these directories is to examine a detailed map of your targeted Search Zone and identify every city, town, and county within the targeted area. Then, using the directory, look up each city, town, and county you identified. Every manufacturer within each city, town and county will be listed, with enough information about each to help you determine whether or not to include it in your Contact List. To purchase a directory, contact the commerce department for your targeted state.

The Business-to-Business Yellow Pages is best used for quickly locating contact information about companies you already know you want to pursue. If you know the name of a specific company and want to know if your Search Zone has a division or branch, using this resource is the fastest (non-computer) way to find out. To acquire information about the specific location, such as the names of the key leaders or what the location does, call the location's switchboard and use the techniques you learned earlier in this program.

Ex-Offender-Friendly Companies

According to the Associated Prisoners Union of America (A.P.U.A), the following major companies are known to hire ex-offenders:

AAMCO Trans	Best Foods	DAP Products
Ace Hardware	Best Western	DelMonte Foods
Alamo Rent-A-Car	BFGoodrich	Delta Air Lines
Alaska Airlines	Black and Decker	Delta Faucets
Allied Van Lines	Blue Cross/Blue Shield	Denny's Inc.
American West Air	Bridgestone/Firestone	Dell Corporation
American Airlines	British Airways	Dole Foods
American Express	Budget Rent-A-Car	Dollar Rent-A-Car
American Greetings	Calvin Klein	Domino's Pizza
Anderson Windows	Campbell Soups	Dow Brands
Apple Computer	Canon USA	Dr Pepper and Snapple
AT&T	Carrier A/C	Dunkin Donuts
ARCO	Casio, Inc.	Dunlop Tires
Atlas Van Lines	Coes-Coin	DuPont Co.
Avis Rent-A-Car	Coldwell Banker	Duracell
Avon Products	Compaq Computer	Eddie Bauer
Bally's	ConAgra Foods	Epson
Baskin-Robbins	Dairy Queen	ExxonMobil

Federal Express	Kmart	Sony
Frito-Lay	Kraft Foods	Southwest Airlines
Fruit of the Loom	Los Angeles Times	Sprint
Fuji Foto	McDonalds	Target
Galoab Toys	New York Times	Toys "R" Us
General Electric	Newsweek	United Airlines
General Mills	Nike	Verizon
GMAC	Pepsi Co	Walmart
Georgia-Pacific	Philip Morris	Yumaha
Hanes Hosiery	Sara Lee	Zerox
Hilton Hotels	Shell	Zenith Electronics
IBM	Showtime Networks	

Military-Friendly Companies

If you are a military veteran, the following companies, and their industries, are known to actively seek out and recruit people with military experience. These companies, along with their competitors, should always be the first companies researched for branches, divisions, plants, or field offices located in your Search Zone:

Abbott	Coca-Cola	Nestle	Procter & Gamble
Aramark	Cott	North American Salt	QVC
Americold Logistics	Edy's Grand	Nucor	Raytheon
Apria Healthcare	GE	Ozburn-Hessey	Target Distribution
BAE	Georgia Pacific	Pepsi	UniFirst
Baxter Healthcare	Grainger	Perrier Group	Unilever
Cardinal Health	LaFarge	Phelps Dodge	Walmart Distribution
Cintas	Nabisco		

Other Companies

You should also include on your Contact List all of the following:

- pharmaceutical manufacturing plants
- corrugated box and packaging plants
- major food processing manufacturing plants
- uniform service companies
- medical device manufacturing plants
- warehousing companies which store and ship perishables
- beverage manufacturing plants and distribution centers
- concrete, cement, and aggregate plants

You can quickly find companies in these categories by doing Internet searches.

Advertisements and Opportunity Leads

Your Contact List should include copies of position advertisements which you found on the Internet, in newspapers, and in publications. These advertisements will all be pursued using the Candidate Contrived Coincidence technique you learned earlier.

Advertised Positions on the Internet

Advertised positions should be printed directly off the websites. These advertisements are found on a company's website, Internet job boards, and in employment websites such as <u>Monster.com</u>, <u>CareerBuilder.com</u>, and <u>www.indeed.com</u>, and similar sites.

When analyzing advertised positions, make certain the positions are located within your Search Zone. Often, corporate websites for large and very large companies will list vacant positions by geography, and just as often they will not. Conversely, if a large or very large company is **headquartered** in your Search Zone, the positions advertised on the corporate website have a significant probability of being at a company site located **outside of your targeted area**. Larger companies do almost all of their online recruiting from their Human Resources departments at corporate headquarters. Nonetheless, unless an advertisement specifically states that a position is located outside of your targeted Search Zone, these advertisements are worth pursuing. It is possible that one or more of the advertised positions is located within your targeted Search Zone.

Briefly research each company, add the appropriate information from each to your Contact List, and then also add a copy of the position advertisements from each company.

Advertised Positions in the Media

Cut out position advertisements in newspapers and magazines from within your Search Zone and add these to your Contact List. You should pursue them in the exact same manner as Internet advertisements, using Candidate Contrived Coincidence. For companies using a "blind" post office box for mailed responses, call the Post Office at the ZIP code indicated in the advertisement. Ask the postal clerk for the name of the company using the box number listed in the advertisement. The Postal Code **requires** the Post Office to release the name of the company. (This will not work for a private advertising box belonging to a newspaper.) For positions advertised on the radio or television, write down the names of the companies, research them, and add them to your Contact List.

Opportunity Leads

People everywhere talk about work, workplaces, and companies. Train yourself to always keep your eyes and ears open to potential opportunities, and especially when in social situations. One of the most common "small talk" topics at social gatherings is careers. When someone mentions a company which is hiring and/or has needs, you should make a mental note of it and then soon thereafter write down the details for possible inclusion in your Contact List. These leads should also be handled using the Candidate Contrived Coincidence technique you use for advertised positions. Never tell others about Candidate Contrived Coincidence or they may use it for themselves.

Scripts for Getting Interviews

As discussed earlier, the telephone is the best tool for obtaining interviews. If you choose to use the telephone to contact business leaders, you need to prepare what you are going to say **before** you make any calls. You should write down and rehearse what you will say so that you can have meaningful exchanges with business leaders, leave effective voicemail messages, set up appointments from voicemail call-backs, and overcome predictable employer responses for delaying moving forward.

The following sections explain what to do. Anything in **bold print** should be written down and kept next to your telephone for easy reference at all times.

Scripts for Speaking With Leaders on the Telephone

You will rarely encounter a cold reception when looking for employment. Everyone you contact who has a job once looked for a job, unless that person was fortunate enough to be born into the family which owns the company in question. This certainly applies when using the telephone effectively in your job search. But you must use it right and be very precise in what you say and do. No streams of consciousness or wandering far from your scripted "pitch" or "presentation." You must impress upon the receiver that you are someone they are interested in talking to and meeting in person. Indeed, you must always strive to speak effectively with such key people, so make certain you write a script or an outline of what you will say before making calls. During your calls, show respect for their time by not engaging in idle talk. Address them as "Mr." or "Ms."

A little rapport building is fine, but get quickly to your pre-written presentation of yourself, which you will learn to construct in this chapter. If you get to the point promptly, the people you are speaking with will see you as a true professional, and they will be helpful. Be sure to write down and plan what you are going to say before you call someone.

Scripts for Voicemail Messages

In an earlier section, you learned how to use the Candidate Contrived Coincidence voicemail technique for advertised positions. **Use that same format for all voicemail presentations**. Write a brief presentation of yourself which is approximately 30 seconds long. Describe the skills, abilities, and experience you have, and also mention the places within an organization where you think you could add value. Close by stating your name, telephone number, and the time period when you will be available or visiting the area where the companies on the Contact List are located. If you are presently living in your Search Zone, say nothing about where you live. That's because if you say in your message that you live in the area, the listener might think they can delay taking action on your call.

When using the Candidate Contrived Coincidence method for advertised positions or known Zone of Opportunities (ZOOs), you should write a separate script for each advertisement you pursue. Each message needs to be tailored as closely as possible to each position or known need without exaggerating your skills, experience, background, and qualifications. Use Candidate Contrived Coincidence for pursuing **all known ZOOs**, whether advertised or not. For example, if you hear a rumor that a company is looking for a certain type of person, write a presentation of yourself which is tailored to that opening.

When not pursuing known openings, you should write a script for a **30-second** basic presentation. This is a general "introduction and attention-grabber" presentation which is intended to generate interest in you.

Below is an example of a basic written presentation for a warehouse supervisor. He has seven years of experience and desires to move near Nashville, Tennessee, where his wife is pursuing her dream of becoming a country music star. This presentation should be deposited in every warehouse manager's voicemail within 30 miles of Nashville:

> *"My name is (name) and I have seven years of experience supervising warehouse operations in high tempo environments. I've worked in consumer products where our products were highly perishable and required timely receiving and shipping, of which I have a lot of experience. I led and mentored up to 40 team members. I'm visiting Nashville the week of (dates) and would really enjoy meeting you while I'm in town. I don't know if you have any present openings or needs right now, but I'm very flexible, will work any shift, and have always outperformed my peers. My name again is (name) and my number is (telephone number). I hope to hear from you. Thanks!"*

When this presentation is made directly to a warehouse manager without the use of voicemail, obviously, you would leave out *"my telephone number is"* and *"I hope to hear from you"* in your presentation. Everything else would remain the same.

Scripts for Converting Contacts Into Interviews

If you deposit between 75 and 150 enthusiastic voicemail messages with leaders, either "Candidate Contrived Coincidence" or "basic," some leaders or their representatives will call you back. These returned calls should generate between four and six interviews for yourself, and that number almost always results in a successful campaign, **but only if you handle those contacts correctly!** When you speak directly with leaders and do not use voicemail, you will also generate interviews, but only if you handle those contacts correctly also!

Handling contacts correctly requires anticipating questions or concerns that could be asked or stated by the leaders you are speaking with. You should prepare written responses, just as your presentation is written, and keep them close at hand.

When a leader returns a voicemail message, it's unlikely they are calling to say the company has no interest in you. Something in the presentation sparked their interest. Also, your voicemail's intent was obvious: seeking meetings for yourself, so the purpose in calling back is likely to be considering whether or not they or someone else at the company should meet with you. They are conducting what is commonly referred to as a "phone screen." A phone screen is used when a leader has a need in mind, a Zone of Opportunity, but doesn't want to waste time meeting people in person who cannot satisfy the need. He might even be unsure exactly what is needed, but it will become clearer once he speaks with the "right" prospective employee. Your purpose is to turn a phone screen into a **face-to-face appointment**. Call-backs will be either from the key executive with whom you left your voicemail or someone he or she directed to return your call. If it's the key executive, which is preferred, that is someone who can discuss Zone of Opportunities which others within the company are unaware of. If the caller was directed to call you, it's usually because he has an open position or need to be filled within his department so the senior executive forwarded your message to him.

When speaking directly with a key leader and not using voicemail, you do not have the voicemail advantages of knowing the contact wishes to speak with you and has an interest in you. In a direct call, you must make your presentation and listen for a response. As with a call-back, however, the contact's response will determine what approach you must take to arrange an interview for yourself.

Either way, whether from a call-back or direct call, you should always try to accomplish five tasks every time you speak with a contact:

1. Draw out potential needs and opportunities.
2. Set an appointment for a face-to-face meeting.
3. Acquire the contact's private email address.
4. Gather additional information about the company, person, opportunity, and hiring process.
5. Get off the telephone!

To do these tasks, you will need to have pre-written scripts close at hand which give good answers to a contact's questions.

When speaking with a leader, your main objective, always, is to arrange a face-to-face meeting. To achieve that, **you need to understand the needs at his company before telling him details about yourself**. The reason for this is simple: if you say one thing about yourself which does not fit his or her need, the conversation will probably be ended. You must ask questions about the organization's needs.

Whether returning your voicemail message or speaking directly with you, a busy person will almost always desire as brief a conversation as possible. He wants to know immediately whether or not you can satisfy the needs of the company, so always expect him to immediately begin asking questions about you. Normally, the first question will be one of two options:

"What are you looking for?" or *"What kind of work do you want to do?"*

It's very dangerous to answer questions directly. If you give an answer which is not exactly what the contact desires, or if you say you are looking for something that differs from what the contact needs, they will terminate the call and you will have lost an excellent opportunity for an interview. However, if you don't answer a direct question in some manner, the contact will think you are evasive. **The best response is to repeat what you said in your presentation describing yourself, then turn the question around to get an understanding of the contact's need(s).**

For example, let's suppose you are the warehouse supervisor desiring to move to Nashville mentioned earlier, and a contact calls back in response to the voicemail message you left him. This person asks, *"What are you looking for?"* You should answer:

> *"Well...I'm pretty flexible. I've been a warehouse supervisor for the past seven years and can excel at a lot of functions, and I am happy doing many things. Maybe I could be of some potential use to your company. What present or potential needs do you have that you may need help with now or in the near future?"*

In this example, you simply restated what you said in your voicemail because obviously something in the voicemail got the contact's attention. Then you turned around the question so that you will gain a clearer understanding of the contact's needs before giving additional details about yourself. This technique ensures that you only give answers that are tailored to the contact's needs.

Write down the scripted responses and always keep it nearby.

A big mistake people make is to answer questions and forget to repeat what they stated in their presentations, and their answers are usually wrong. For example, the leader asks, *"What do you want to do?"* An ineffective job seeker would answer:

> *"I'm open to doing a lot of things, but I have been very happy as a warehouse supervisor so that's probably where I would fit best. What do you need?"*

The contact responds,

> *"Well, I need a warehouse scheduler (a position a warehouse supervisor could excel at), not a supervisor, so you probably won't be happy here, but thanks for calling anyway. Good-bye."*

Do not make that common mistake! Write down your response ahead of time and thus be prepared for the *"What are you looking for?"* question.

If you turn the question around effectively, most managers will respond by either telling you of a need at their company or by saying,

> *"We might have some needs in some areas, but I would need to know more about you to know if you would fit. **Can you send me your resume?"***

Requesting a resume is a very common response. However, when a resume is sent without first arranging an interview or having a pre-set time to review the resume over the telephone with the employer, it is far easier for the employer to never get around to actually scheduling a meeting with you. For that reason, you must consider a request for a resume as an opportunity to begin a conversation with the contact, a chance to build rapport, and to identify needs.

You should respond,

> *"Sure. What is your confidential email address?"*

The executive will not hesitate to give you his confidential email address because you are accommodating his request. At this point, you have achieved one of your five objectives: you have acquired the executive's private email address. That alone opens a door for continuous future communication with this person. Now you should attempt to **get the conversation back toward the needs of his organization.** Say this:

> *"I will get that resume off to you later today. Mr. Smith, what are some of the potential areas you have needs in?"*

The executive will give either a detailed or very brief answer. Then you should try to keep the conversation going by asking questions about his or her business, such as:

> *"Mr. Smith, can you tell me a little bit about your warehouse? What do you ship from there, and to what customers?"*

Your goal is to keep the contact talking. That may sound difficult to do, but in most cases it won't be if you focus on the needs of the organization and how you may be able to help. Most business leaders will remain interested in continuing the conversation with you if they think you have something to offer. If you can keep the contact talking, and building rapport, there's a good chance you can close the conversation with a scheduled appointment to meet this person. You will be surprised by how often a contact forgets about asking for a resume and moves directly to a meeting.

While speaking with the contact, always be looking for the earliest opportunity to **set up an interview.** Setting up an interview is the objective of the call, and you **must** stay focused on that goal. At the earliest "right' moment, you should say something like this:

> *"Sounds like an exciting place. I'm sure I'd like to meet with you and see your organization. I have a proposal for you: I'm looking at my schedule for when I'm in your town, and I'm free all day on the (date) and the morning of the (a different date). Why don't we arrange a brief initial meeting for one of those two dates?"*

If the executive responds by asking a second time for the resume, do not make another attempt to keep the conversation going. Politely terminate the call by saying that you will email the resume later that day, **but ask him for a specific time you can call him back during the following day to discuss your resume with him.**

If the contact does not object to your proposal to meet with you, then assume that he agrees to the meeting! Suggest a day and time to meet. Verify the location where you will have the meeting, and tell him that you will email your resume so he receives it prior to the interview.

The usual sequence for taking a presentation to an interview involves the following:

The Presentation Sequence

1. You make either a voicemail or direct presentation of yourself.
2. A call-back is received from either a business leader or his representative.
3. He asks, *"What kind of work do you want to do?"*
4. You respond with a rephrasing of what you said in the voicemail.
5. You ask, *"What present or potential needs do you have?"*
6. Keep the conversation focused on the needs of the organization.
7. Ask for a meeting at the earliest "right" moment in the conversation.

You now have an appointment for yourself and have accomplished your major objective. If the contact needs to get off the telephone, you still have an interview, so don't try to keep him on the phone any longer. However, in order to increase the chances of receiving an offer of employment from this company, you now need to gather information. The more information you have, the better your prospects for a successful interview. The best way to transition into information gathering is to say something like this:

"(Contact's name), is there anything you can tell me at this time which would help me prepare for our meeting, so I make the best use of your time when we meet? If this isn't a good time, that's OK, and we can simply discuss that when we meet."

Remember, most business leaders will probably want to get off the phone as soon as they have scheduled an appointment with you, so do not press any issue if they say they do not have time at that moment and must get off the phone. Also, you do not want this conversation to evolve into a **telephone interview** because if you give one incorrect answer, that could also cause a cancellation of your meeting. You must balance risking your interview with gathering information so you will be prepared for your meeting, so always ask the question above. If the leader is in a conversational mood, here are some good questions to ask:

What do you see as your primary area of need in your organization right now?"

What areas within (functional area discussed) do you see as having problems?

What is the biggest problem you see as needing a solution?

In your view, what are the three most important functions of the position? (Ask this question only if you have been told there is an open position.)

Whom would this position report to?

Can I meet with him/her while I'm visiting the facility on (day)?

How many people do you have in your plant (or at your site)?

What do you manufacture/ship at your plant/warehouse?

How many shifts does your plant run?

What shift would this position be?

Do you have PLCs (programmable logic controllers) in your plant?

What kinds of equipment would I work on? (Ask only if the business leader told you he needs a technician . . . and if that's what you are.)

Ask the following questions only if the leader is very agreeable and friendly:

(Name), what is your background? How long have you been with (company)?

Were you ever in the military? (Ask only if you are a military veteran.)

What is the most important thing you look for when interviewing someone?

Where there are many more questions you could ask, these are some of the most important ones. By the time you get through three or four questions, the prospect will probably begin to show signs that he or she wants to get off the phone, and you should stop asking questions at that point. However, ask as many questions as the business leader will allow you to ask. Often, business leaders enjoy speaking about themselves and their companies, especially if they founded the company and built it up from humble beginnings, and many want to share their stories. That occurs often when speaking with the owners of privately owned companies. Write down all of the questions listed above, and ask them if you feel you have good rapport with the person with whom you are speaking.

Now you have only one objective left on the call . . . **get off the phone!** Staying on the telephone too long is always a bad idea, and is often worse than hanging up too soon. You can talk yourself right out of your scheduled appointment with the business leader. You **must** end the call before you inadvertently say something that causes the business leader to reconsider his/her appointment with you.

It is extremely frustrating to have a confirmed appointment and then hear the leader say, *"On second thought, maybe we should sit tight on a meeting . . . I'll call you later next week if we're interested in going further."* A good fishing analogy would be to have a large fish on your line, get him into the boat, and then he flops overboard and swims away as you attempted to take a picture of him. **Always** get off the telephone when you have what you need.

Within 24 hours after the call, you should send an email to the leader. In the email, you should attach your **customized resume** as a Microsoft Word or PDF document, and the resume should be developed by using the information you gathered in your conversation with the leader. (That is why you should ask the questions listed above). Also, write something about what you plan to do in preparation for the meeting. That way, the business leader will know you are going to expend some effort in preparation for the meeting and will be less likely to cancel on you (if he/she is considerate, that is). You should also restate in the email the date and time of the interview. Here is a sample email script:

Dear (contact's name);

It was a pleasure speaking with you today (yesterday).

Attached is my resume, and I am looking forward to meeting you on (date) at (time) to discuss (name of company) and how I could possibly contribute to its success. I am a problem-solver type of person and am excited about challenges, and I will formulate some possible solutions for the areas of needs you mentioned. In the interim, if you need anything from me or have any questions for me, please do not hesitate to contact me. Thank you.

Sincerely and respectfully,

(Your name, telephone number, and email address)

Handling Common Concerns

Some leaders will be genuinely interested in you yet delay making a commitment to meet with you. Delaying commitments is human nature, and it can be frustrating for you. Anytime a leader delays scheduling an appointment with you, it means he/she has a "concern." Some concerns do not even seem like problems, but they are. Skill at handling common concerns expressed by leaders is crucial to setting up appointments. The three most common concerns, expressed in the following statements, include:

I need to see your resume before I schedule an interview with you.

We have no openings at the present time.

You need to speak with Human Resources.

You will learn how to address each of these concerns as well as prepare scripts for handling each.

The statements above are the most common initial responses from business leaders when speaking with a job hunter on the telephone. You may hear them often. The statements also seem to show sincere interest on the leader's part. Most often, however, the leader is simply saying the first thing that comes into his/her mind in the conversation, i.e., a "knee jerk" reaction. For that reason, there is something you should learn to do when you hear any of the three statements above:

Wait until the leader says the same concern twice before addressing it.

What that means is you must learn to politely ignore concerns the first time you hear them. That's because when you are presenting yourself over the telephone to a leader, he is probably not really "hearing" what you are saying. That applies even if what you said impacts positively a Zone of Opportunity within the mind of the leader, and he allowed it to go right over his head. For that reason, you must practice ignoring a concern until you hear the same concern a **second time**. That is an unnatural act for most people because most believe it is rude to ignore something spoken. However, with practice, ignoring a concern can easily be accomplished without appearing rude.

Here is an example of how a leader, a **potential employer**, might respond to you, a **potential candidate**:

Employer: *You sound like you have a great background, but I would like to see your resume before I schedule an interview with you.*

Candidate: *I understand. Do you have a need right now for someone with my background?* (Concern ignored.)

Employer: *Well, yes . . . I do need someone like you. I need someone to run my warehouse because my warehouse manager just resigned from the company.*

Candidate: *Wow! That's exactly what I have been doing for the last seven years with my present company, and also in your industry. I am visiting your area on Tuesday and Wednesday of next week. I would love to meet with you while I'm in town.*

Employer: *Well, I guess we could meet if you're visiting our town.* (Candidate arranges time and date for the meeting).

Notice how the "concern" of needing to see a resume before arranging an interview was ignored by the candidate and it simply went away. The concern was **invalid**, something the employer stated off the top of his or her head, something not entirely true, but not entirely false either. The concern went away because the candidate shifted the conversation toward the **needs of the employer** rather than towards a discussion of the candidate's resume. Had the candidate started discussing his resume instead of the employer's needs, the result would have been a discussion about resumes instead of needs, and the outcome would have been entirely different.

Here's the general rule of thumb for dealing with possible objections to meeting with you at this stage of your job search:

When a business leader states the same concern twice, it becomes a **valid concern**, and if it is ignored a second time, the business leader will become irritated.

The following example demonstrates a different outcome: in reference to a candidate's attempt to ignore the employer's concerns:

Employer: *You sound like you have a great background, but I'd like to see your resume before I schedule an interview with you.*

Candidate: *I understand. Mr. Smith, do you have a need right now for someone with my background?*

Employer: *Well, yes . . . I do need someone like you. I need someone to run my warehouse because my warehouse manager just resigned.*

Candidate: *Wow! That's exactly what I have been doing for the last seven years with my present company, and also in your industry. I am visiting your area on Tuesday and Wednesday of next week. I would love to meet with you while I'm in town.*

Employer: *I would like that, but as I said, I need to see your resume first before scheduling something.*

If the potential candidate continues to ignore this concern and attempts again to schedule a meeting, the potential employer may become angry. Ignoring something twice IS rude. The candidate **must** deal with this concern because it was mentioned twice and it is a **valid** concern.

Always wait until you hear the same concern twice before addressing it. You will be amazed at how often a concern simply goes away when you focus your discussion on the needs of the potential employer rather than the concern that he/she stated.

The following scripts are very effective for overcoming each of the three most common employer concerns we outlined on page 55.

1. **A script for responding to an employer's *insistence on reviewing your resume* prior to scheduling an interview:**

   Employer: *As I said, I'd really like to take a look at your resume before setting up an interview.*

   Candidate: *I will get one off to you today. What is your email address?* (He gives it.) *Now, what areas within your company do you see some potential needs?*

If the potential employer says he doesn't know of any needs right now, it is unlikely you will receive an interview, but your resume will be in his email and will become a "planted seed" nonetheless, so you should send it. On the other hand, if the employer says he has a need, ask him for some basic information about the need. After acquiring some basic information, end the call by asking for a time on **the very next day** when you can call him to discuss your resume. In the unlikely event he does not wish to set a time, it means he is not very serious about you as a potential candidate for employment.

If he gives you a time to call him, you should email him right away a resume that is **tailored to his need by using the information he gave you**. Use the email as your cover letter and refer to the conversation you and he had. Attach your tailored resume as a Word document. For the "subject" line of the email, put "(Your name)'s resume, as requested."

The reason you should ask for a time the next day to discuss your resume is that your chances of receiving an interview always diminish rapidly with each day that passes after emailing a resume. Also, you have accommodated his request for your resume and the least he can do is discuss it with you, and so he probably will agree to do so. When you discuss it with him the next day, and if things go well, at the conclusion of the discussion ask him directly, *"Can we now set a date and time to meet?"*

2. **A script for when a potential employer says there are "no openings" at the company:**

Employer: *As I said, we just don't have any openings right now.*

Candidate: *(Name), well, I really didn't expect you to have any openings. I just wanted to introduce myself in such a way that you would remember me for future opportunities. I am very goal-oriented and go after the things I really want. Other than openings, is there any area within your company where you would add someone if someone who was strong enough came along?*

3. **A script you can use when a potential employer instructs you to "go to Human Resources":**

Employer: *As I said, you need to go to Human Resources.*

Candidate: *Who is the Director (or Manager) of Human Resources? (Name is given.) Can I tell (name of HR person) that we spoke and that you might have an interest in meeting with me?*

In the unlikely event the employer responds with *"No, I'd rather not have you say that to the Human Resources people,"* you should reply:

If I cannot get through to (name of HR person), can I call you back?

The employer will respond with either *"Yes, call me back"* or *"I will contact them and make sure they are ready to speak with you."* Either way, this puts you in a good position. The Human Resources people will know you are important to the employer if he calls them. If he does not call them, the chances are high that they will ignore your call because they get bombarded by job applicants. This opens a door to deal directly with the employer, which is preferred anyway.

Dealing through Human Resources as a job seeker is almost always a nonproductive exercise in futility at most companies. Most Human Resources departments are understaffed and overworked, are constantly approached by job seekers, and are flooded with resumes. Whenever possible, you should try to set up interviews without the involvement of Human Resources. If you are required by the employer to go through Human Resources, always ask the employer for the name of the highest ranking Human Resources person on site. That should at least help you navigate the Human Resources maze.

Whenever you hear from Human Resources **after** an interview, take that as a **good** sign. It means the employer wants to proceed to the next step with you. The employer would not have instructed Human Resources to make contact with you if he was not interested in proceeding.

Basic Resumes and Tailored Resumes

The fourth and final component of your Campaign Plan focuses on your resume. Included in subsequent pages are examples of a basic resume and resume versions which have been tailored to specific opportunities. A basic resume is the resume you will prepare containing all your experience. It is from that resume which you will make customized changes for pursuing specific opportunities. Customized resumes are always targeted to the opportunity pursued.

A poorly written resume hurts your chances for gaining interviews. Effective writing means **removing** anything that does not add to your desirability and **adding** anything that adds desirability – without ever misrepresenting anything about you. As an example, if you are sending your resume to a potential employer at a manufacturing plant for a manufacturing position, you should use the information given to you in your conversation with the employer to customize your basic resume to what the employer said he was looking for.

The two examples on pages 61-62 are the actual resumes used by a 30/30 placement professional to place an engineering candidate into a manufacturing position with a major food processing company (name and contact information altered). Using the Candidate Contrived Coincidence method for pursuing an advertised position the company was running on its website, the placement professional was called back by the manufacturing plant general manager in response to the voicemail he'd left him which described the candidate in a way that closely matched the advertised position requirements.

Using the actual words from the position advertisement, and also some of the general manager's own stated requirements for the position, the 30/30 professional tailored this candidate's resume to reflect exactly what the company wanted, without misrepresenting anything about the candidate. To do this required rearranging the resume and dropping things from the resume which would not help the candidate. Most significantly, a resume which presented a "Sales Engineer" was rewritten to present a "Manufacturing Engineer."

The 30/30 placement professional used two resume versions for this candidate's campaign – one for pursuing manufacturing opportunities, and the other for pursuing sales opportunities. The resume on page 61 is tailored for manufacturing opportunities. The resume on page 62 is tailored for sales positions. Compare the two and notice the differences between them.

The second resume, customized for sales positions, reflects what the candidate was doing at the time he was in the 30/30 process. Even though this candidate called himself a "Sales Engineer," there was nothing deceptive about dropping the word "Sales" from his resume when pursuing manufacturing opportunities. That's because a "Sales Engineer" is, in fact, a type of "Engineer," so it remained truthful to drop the word "Sales" and keep "Engineer". The resume for manufacturing was also written to accent only those functions the candidate performed in his sales position which were mentioned in the position advertisement, and everything related to sales activities was minimized.

Worth re-emphasizing is the fact that everything on both resumes was something the candidate had done, even if it had to be added to his resume. That way, both resumes remained 100% truthful, yet each presented a different type of candidate for different types of opportunities.

A reader of a resume will make his/her own judgments as to what the person does. Tailoring a resume requires the ability to express your background and experience in such a way as to reflect only what an employer is looking for. To do that means you must first understand the needs of the employer. Anything on a resume that adds something which you are not certain is what the employer is looking for is a potential interview killer. For example, adding "pursuing my master's degree while working full time" sounds like a positive. It isn't a positive for many business leaders, who will view that as meaning you will need time off to take exams.

Finally, never use a functional resume format unless absolutely necessary, such as if you are re-entering the job market after a long absence. While such resumes primarily emphasize transferable skills and accomplishments, they leave out critical chronological employment information employers look for – the who, what, where, and when of a candidate's employment experience.

Many ex-offenders use functional resumes, because they need to de-emphasize obvious employment time gaps while incarcerated. While that's okay, do know that such resumes have limitations, especially with potential employers who closely scrutinize resumes for names, dates, and places as they search for patterns of accomplishments or possible red flags. Unfortunately, few employers spent much time reading functional resumes. Many assume the candidate is hiding something, such as his/her age or lack of relevant work experience. (It is better to be older and proud of it than try to hide it). If you use a functional resume, be prepared to answer questions concerning your progressive – or lack thereof – work history.

In our experience, most resume readers also want to know where you have been and what you have done more so than what you claim you can do. They look for **patterns of employment** as well as evidence of **employment advancement**, which are indicated in a chronology of employment dates, positions, and employers. If you use a functional resume, be prepared to explain exactly what you have done in the pass in terms of specific employers, positions, skills, and accomplishments. If you've been incarcerated, you'll need to develop a compelling story about your rehabilitation and transformation – why someone should hire you rather than someone without a rap sheet. For information on how to best do that, see Ron's two ex-offender re-entry books: *The Ex-Offender's Quick Job Hunting Guide* and *The Ex-Offender's New Job Finding and Survival Guide* (see pages 121 and 124).

JOHN F. JACKSON
18 Snowbound Road
Topsfield, MA 01983
(978) 555- 2714

BSME	University of Lowell, Lowell, MA	1999
MBA	Thomas College, Waterville, ME	2003
PE	Professional Engineer, #87963	2005

KOWLSON MACHINE ENGINEERING, Andover, MA (Manufacturer of custom design process machinery and capital equipment for a variety of industries)   **2011-present**
Engineer (liaison between customer, engineering, and production)
- Visit customer manufacturing plant and identify customer machinery needs, design machine concept for solution, interface with and coordinate the production of the machines in our production facility (a modern machine shop), supervise and follow through on machinery installation at customer site
- "Point person" for customer technical inquiries, problem solving, and mechanical engineering back up
- Provide engineering support to a variety of industries and manufacturing processes
- Write proposals for design, engineering and manufacture of custom built production machinery
- Responsible for refining and developing relationships with over 200 customers since joining the company

DIAMOND PHOENIX CORPORATION, Bath, ME   **2010-2011**
Manufacturing Project Engineer, Maintenance Manager, Safety and Environmental Coordinator
(Reason for leaving: major plant-wide RIF)
- Performed engineering tasks and supervised maintenance and production crews in PLC driven chemical process and coatings facility
- Supervised plant construction projects as customer's project engineer to contractors
- Authored "Safety and Environmental Policies" manual to EPA/OSHA code for 120 employees
- Put in service a $750,000 powder coating chemical process facility, integrated and tuned controls for product uniformity, optimized chemistry efficiency, stabilized equipment's reliability
- Solved coating problem creating a savings of $375,000/yr, by substituting plating with powder coating
- Wore many "hat." Performed three jobs simultaneously due to adverse economic conditions affecting our plant

MEAD PAPER COMPANY, Bucksport Mill, Bucksport, ME   **2007-2010**
Senior Process Control Engineer (Paper Mill Group)
- Directed 14 technicians and 80 operators in operating and troubleshooting PLCs
- Managed, configured, and prioritized process control services in paper mill
- Installed new control system configuration on 10-day paper machine rebuild ($2.9M capital)
- Implemented alkaline conversion controls: CIO2, water and fiber segregation, pH controls ($1.9M capital)

INTERNATIONAL PAPER COMPANY, Androscoggin Mill, Jay, ME   **1999-2007**
Process Control Engineer / Senior Production Foreman / Maintenance Engineer
- Diagnosed problem and implemented paper winding controls ($1.3 M/yr. Loss reduction
- Coordinated improvement efforts of contract control service providers (Measurex, ABB)
- Reduced labor costs 37% while increasing pulp production 20% in 2 years
- Eliminated repetitive equipment failures: pumps, conveyors, piping systems
- Planned, coordinated, and contracted repairs to wide variety of process equipment and systems
- Developed NDT programs, to assure compliance of pressure vessels and hazardous piping systems

COMPUTER SKILLS: MS Office, AS-400, Honeywell, Allen Bradley, Moore, PI, and Msx PLCs

JOHN F. JACKSON
18 Snowbound Road
Topsfield, MA 01983
(978) 555- 2714

SUMMARY
Masters Degree in Business Administration plus engineering degree, plus fourteen years of experience in finding solutions to customer problems in both sales and manufacturing environments.

BSME	University of Lowell, Lowell, MA	1999
MBA	Thomas College, Waterville, ME	2003
PE	Professional Engineer, #87963	2005

KOWLSON MACHINE ENGINEERING, Andover, MA (Manufacturer of custom build process machinery and capital equipment for a variety of industries)   2011-present
Sales Engineer
- Identify, contact, and call on new and existing industrial clients. Identify needs, provide customer de-signed and built machinery solutions. Sell to CEOs, plant managers, engineering managers, and executives in large and small companies
- Call on a variety of industries and manufacturing processes
- Write proposals for design, engineering and manufacture of custom machinery, machining, fabrication
- Technical and commercial interface for company, define problems, develop solutions
- Develop and maintain marketing literature, develop and conduct customer presentations
- Developed over 200 customers since joining the company

DIAMOND PHOENIX CORPORATION, Bath, ME (plant RIF)   2010-2011
Manufacturing / Project Engineer, Maintenance Manager, Safety and Environmental Coordinator
- Supervised maintenance and production crews
- Scoped, awarded and managed contractor projects
- Developed, implemented, and managed "Safety and Environmental policies" to code for 120 employees
- Put in service a $750,000 powder coating facility, integrated and tuned controls for product uniformity, optimized chemistry efficiency, stabilized equipment's reliability
- Solved coating problem creating a savings of $375,000/yr, by substituting plating with powder coating
- Wore three "hats" simultaneously due to adverse economic conditions affecting our industry and facility

MEAD PAPER COMPANY, Bucksport Mill, Bucksport, ME   2007-2010
Senior Process Control Engineer (Paper Mill Group)
- Directed 14 technicians and 80 operators
- Troubleshot and improved processes and control systems
- Managed, configured, and prioritized process control services in paper mill
- Installed new control system configuration on 10-day paper machine rebuild ($2.9M capital)
- Implemented alkaline conversion controls: CIO2, water and fiber segregation, pH controls ($1.9M capital)

INTERNATIONAL PAPER COMPANY, Androscoggin Mill, Jay, ME   1999-2007
Process Control Engineer / Senior Production Foreman / Maintenance Engineer
- Diagnosed problem and implemented paper winding controls ($1.3 M/yr. Loss reduction)
- Coordinated improvement efforts of contract control service providers (Measurex, ABB)
- Reduced labor costs 37% while increasing pulp production 20% in 2 years
- Eliminated repetitive equipment failures: pumps, conveyors, piping systems
- Planned, coordinated, and contracted repairs to wide variety of process equipment and systems
- Developed NDT programs, to assure compliance of pressure vessels and hazardous piping systems

COMPUTER SKILLS:
MS Office, AS-400 – VMS bus applications. Control Systems: Honeywell, Allen Bradley, Moore, PI, and Msx PLCs

Email as Your Primary Contact List Strategy

Up to this point in this program, you have been creating scripts and materials for use primarily during **telephone** contact with employers. Even though the telephone and voicemail are by far the most effective tools for generating interviews, many who use this program are not going to want to use the telephone for working through their Contact List. That's not a problem because, as was mentioned earlier, this program can be effective without using the telephone for making initial contact with employers.

Other than voicemail, the second best method for making initial contact with employers is email. Using the methods discussed in Chapter 3 for finding the best email addresses of employers, you should construct and send to employers an email message about yourself which is brief, informative, and interesting. The following is a good example of an email used by a machine shop supervisor to send to owners of machine shops located within his Search Zone:

> Mr. (Name):
>
> My name is Bill Smith and I have ten years of experience running machine shops. I have solid experience with all kinds of high tech CNC machining equipment as well as low tech manual machines, and supervising machinists who operate and maintain such equipment. I am moving to (name of location where the shop is) and visiting for job hunting the week of (dates) and would enjoy meeting you to discuss what I can bring to a machining operation. I don't know if you have any present or potential needs right now, but I promise you I will not waste your time. I can be reached at this email address or the following telephone number (number). I hope to hear from you.
>
> Respectfully,
>
> Bill Smith

It is important to note a few things about this email. First, a resume is not attached to the email. The purpose of this email is not to introduce a resume; rather, it is to engage the recipient in a conversation and not have the person simply look at it and decide to either file it away or delete it. When a resume is attached, recipients tend to look at the resume and decide in an instant whether or not to meet the person, and that decision will not change. Second, the email is brief. Busy people receive dozens of emails and want to move through them quickly. A lengthy email very likely will be screened out by a spam filter, or skimmed by the recipient and deleted as too long to read. Finally, the email mentions an opportunity to get together which will not cost the recipient money for travel and lodging. (If the sender lives in the Search Zone, the sender would have written *"I am taking the week of _____ to meet with machine shop owners."*)

In order to generate a sufficient number of meetings with business leaders for employment to result, you will need to send a lot of emails. Historically with this program, if you send 75 emails, you will generate between seven and ten responses, from which you should receive four to seven meetings. That is enough meetings for a successful 30/30 outcome.

Email is an excellent means for making contact if you are hesitant to use the telephone. Once you have made contact, however, you will still need to speak on the phone with the employers who reply.

5

Action

"Getting job interviews requires a very systematic and disciplined approach to implementing your 30/30 job search."

DURING THE ACTION PHASE, you implement the plan you organized in Phase I over a well focused four-day period. The Campaign Plan is your overall roadmap. The majority of your time during this phase will be spent contacting the companies and people you listed on your Contact List. Your primary objective during Phase II is to schedule interviews with potential employers, who may or may not have job openings.

Success is Just Six Companies Away

Numbers count if you work this process according to plan and work the details of implementation. Based on our experience with hundreds of clients using the 30/30 job search process, we know what works and doesn't work. Here are the facts of 30/30 job search life. Unless you have a very unusual profile, if you meet with six different companies, you'll have a high probability of getting hired. Historically, such meetings have translated into an 83-percent probability of success. If you meet with seven companies, the probability of getting hired increases to 97 percent. If you meet with only four companies, you still have a 73-percent probability of a successful outcome.

However, these percentages for success are only valid if you correctly implement every step in the 30/30 job search process. If not, the percentages will go down. Whatever you do, don't short-change yourself by trying to modify this process by failing to follow our seasoned advice on how to make this process work for you. You **must** implement properly. So just do it!

Use Your Job Search Time Wisely

Obtaining interviews requires a systematic, focused, and disciplined approach that uses time wisely. You work this phase of your job search during the hours of a typical business workday, 8am to 5pm. In the job placement industry we commonly refer to this as a **balanced day**. A balanced day means that you start each day knowing what you are going to do and when you are going to do it, with **no wasted time.** A typical balanced day looks like this:

8:00am - 9:00am:	Adjust plan and answer emails
9:00am - 12:00noon:	Make contact with companies and employers
12:00noon - 1:00pm:	Lunch
1:00pm - 3:00pm:	Make contact with companies and employers
3:00pm - 5:00pm:	Prepare and mail letters to employers

During your balanced day, you work through your Contact List during a normal eight-hour workday or after hours. If you work at this during the day, you should work at it full time. People who fail at this program do so mostly because they waste time and do not have the **discipline** to execute their Contact List. Your level of discipline will be related to how motivated you are to obtain employment.

During Phase I, you developed your Contact List with a list of companies and the names of the potential employers to contact at those companies. As we noted earlier, that list should contain, at a minimum, 75-150 companies. You should now break up the list into "blocks" of companies and people to contact over the course of four days, not six or seven days. The time allotted for each phase of the 30/30 program is the maximum amount of time you should spend on that phase, and you will want to have time in reserve in case something unexpected puts you behind schedule. If you complete making it through your Contact List in four days, you will have time later on in the program to search out even more companies to contact, and that increases the chances of more interviews.

Working in Time Blocks

In order to work successfully with your Contact List, break your tasks into manageable periods – time blocks. Begin by breaking up your list of companies into an equal number of companies and employers to contact each day between 9am and 12pm and between 1pm and 3pm. These time frames will become your most productive periods. For example, if your Contact List has 80 total companies on it, then make contact with the employers at 20 companies per day over four days – 10 companies in the morning, 10 in the afternoon. Keeping your activities in time blocks will add structure to your day and keep you on schedule.

Contact Sequencing

Everyone who makes contact with strangers needs to warm up before doing so. This applies whether you are in a sales setting or going to a party. If you are disciplined enough to use voicemail as your main strategy, which is the most effective tool for job hunting, make your first few voicemails with companies which seem on the surface to have the fewest needs. Call the mom-and-pop businesses first. After all, if you perform poorly in your presentations, you are doing so with those who are least likely to hire you anyway. Also, you will refine your presentation as you warm up. Practicing in this manner will help you sound confident later on when calling a company with advertised positions or a known need.

Always schedule your Candidate Contrived Coincidence calls between 11am and noon. You should be thoroughly warmed up, confident, and well prepared to the situation. When you leave voicemails for known needs, your messages will sound strong. Also, many employers retrieve their messages at noon. When you return from lunch, make your first few calls after lunch the same way – to companies which probably will not have significant needs. However, be forewarned of the unexpected.

NEVER make a call to any company with the assumption there will not be the potential for an interview. Make every call with your best, most enthusiastic effort! Do not lose an opportunity for an interview because your presentation was unenthusiastic.

If you are making your voicemail calls after business hours, you will encounter companies where you cannot leave voicemail. Accordingly, make as many calls as you can, even if that means moving into the next day's list of companies on your Contact List.

Adjusting Your Plan

It is well known in business and in life that **nothing** ever goes as planned, and that a plan is only good until the moment you attempt to implement it. This is also true for those in 30/30 programs. For example, you could be interrupted for a family matter, or you find that some companies on your Contact List no longer exist. Expect to make continuous tweaks and adjustments to your plan as you work through it – adding a contact here, dropping one there. However, do not allow setbacks to hold up your progress. Keep working!

Best Interview Times

When arranging interviews, you should always try to meet with potential employers whenever and wherever they want to do so. However, if you are given an opportunity to choose the time and place for a meeting, certain days and times tend to yield better results from interviews.

The worst day of the week to schedule an interview is Monday.

For example, the worst day of the week to schedule an interview is Monday. That's when employers are distracted and trying to get their minds back into their work after a weekend. If you must have an interview on a Monday, make it for later in the day, preferably after 3pm.

The best day of the week for an interview is Thursday. Most people are beginning to look forward to the weekend, are in a better mood, and the most important thing of all is this: Friday is the next day. If your meeting goes well on Thursday, you will be in an excellent position to continue the discussion the very next day, possibly securing for yourself an offer of employment by the end of the day on Friday.

Most hires occur on Fridays, and most interview processes require at least two interviews.

Tuesday and Wednesday are okay for interviews, but they are not as effective as Thursday.

Many interviewers desire to meet someone either before or after working hours. Breakfast and lunch interviews are fine, but when you are on one of these interviews, always keep in mind that there is only about one hour to get a lot of work done because the interviewer is going to have to get back to the office. Dinner interviews are better than breakfast interviews because there usually isn't an impending deadline.

If you have the good fortune of having more than one interview coming up, and you have a say about when the interviews are to occur, always schedule the company which seems to have the greatest needs for the middle of your interviewing order. By that time, you should have some good interviewing experience, the interviewing jitters will subside, and you will perform at your best. Here is our recommended interview scheduling for each day of the week:

Effective Interview Scheduling

Monday: The worst day; schedule companies that are least likely to hire

Tuesday: Morning is okay; afternoon is better

Wednesday: Morning is okay; afternoon is better

Thursday: The best day of the week; schedule companies with urgent employment needs

Friday: Try to keep open for second interviews from earlier in week

Appendices A and B include detailed discussions of interviewing principles.

6

Getting Hired

"Focus on acing the interview, accepting an offer, and getting started on the right foot from day one."

THIS IS THE MOST CRITICAL phase of your job search – it's where success or failure is determined. And success depends heavily upon whether or not you carefully follow the 30/30 approach to interviewing and accepting job offers. You need to pay particular attention to the hiring details outlined in this chapter.

Nine Actions You Need to Take

You need to do the following things during this important phase of your job search:

1. **Prepare for interviews by researching thoroughly each company and each person interviewing you.** You should read and follow the interview principles revealed in Appendix A (pages 79-101), and role-play, rehearse, and practice interview question responses and scripts until you can respond without sounding like you are reciting from memory, rehearsed, and scripted.

2. **Ask your interviewers intelligent questions**, but **not** about pay, vacation, benefits, or other personal issues, unless the employer brings them up. Check out our sample questions in Appendix B (pages 109-110).

3. **Negotiate an employment offer which is reasonable** – if the opportunity to negotiate arises. By "reasonable" we mean something equal to what you were last earning if unemployed, and no more than 10 percent better than what you presently earn if employed. You will also not ask for more than two changes to any original offer.

4. **Provide contact information for references** from former direct supervisors, **not** from friends and family members.

5. **Accept with enthusiasm a verbal offer that is acceptable to you.** Do this before receiving a written offer. Don't make the mistake of asking for the written offer before making any decisions. Do not take more than 24 hours to decide on any offer.

6. **Establish a start date** and immediately begin accomplishing all pre-employment tasks such as a physical examination.

7. **Report for work on the date you agreed**, and arrive 20 minutes prior to the required time for arrival.

8. **Spend your first weeks on the job listening and learning** rather than making big changes or a "splash." The only exception is if your supervisor has specifically instructed you to take charge with a "strong arm" approach in order to fix serious organizational problems.

9. **Avoid asking for or taking any time off, or leaving work early** except for true emergencies during your first six weeks of employment.

Prepare for Job Interviews

Once you have scheduled a job interview or a meeting with an employer, you should carefully study the interviewing principles outlined in Appendix A. Many of these principles may be familiar to you; others will be new, such as the "Interview Closing Sequence." Do your best to learn the scripts and pointers in Appendix A.

Next, start researching the company and its people, products, and services. This is where your research skills will pay off. Go to the company's website and read every page. Web pages are the easiest sources of company information today, and lack of familiarity with a company's website will immediately kill your chances of success during an interview.

After examining a company's website, do more research by using Internet search engines (start with Google.com, DuckDuckGo.com, Bing.com, Ask.com, Mahalo.com, Dogpile.com, Yahoo.com) and seek out information about the company's press releases, key people, and anything else you can find. The most important information relates to the people you will meet – both personal and professional information. Acquiring this information is key to establishing a positive relationship with interviewers, appearing likable, and communicating your interest – three of the most important factors in getting hired. For example, if you know an interviewer is an accomplished musician, has written a book, or has given a speech recently, mentioning those accomplishments in the interview at appropriate moments can help establish a very favorable connection with the interviewer.

When is the right moment to bring up during an interview things you learned from your research about the interviewer? The right moment is that point in time where you say something which pleasantly surprises the interviewer. For example, don't let on early in an interview that you know the interviewer's son qualified to try out for the Olympics at his college. When the interview progresses to hobbies and leisure activities, say something like *"I enjoy watching competitive collegiate sporting events, like the meet where your son beat three other potential Olympians to qualify for the Olympic trials in swimming."* This type of "insider" information is often found by conducting in-depth research on the Internet.

You'll find numerous resources for researching companies and people. If you want to do lengthy research, do so. However, it's also important that you not over-prepare for an interview. That's because you will be very disappointed if, after working extremely hard preparing for an interview, it turns out to be a very short meeting, a mismatch, or an "empty interview" in which the interviewer says at the outset that there will not be any chance for an offer. The Internet alone is sufficient for obtaining enough information about companies and people for interview success. Do the appropriate research, but do not "over-work."

Role Playing, Rehearsing, and Practicing Answers to Interview Questions

Many job hunting books recommend that candidates arrive at interviews prepared with great answers for just about any and all possible interview questions. In fact, these books often provide what they claim to be the "best" answers to interview questions. Unfortunately, interviewers recognize "canned" answers immediately and are put off by them. (They have read the books themselves.) Also, most interviewers are turned off by candidates who seem overly confident or appear too smooth or rehearsed. Interviewers want to hire "real" people – those who interview well, but not come across as slick and glib. They want people who are human beings, not expert interviewers.

> *The most important information you should gather relates to the people you will meet – both personal and professional*

People are hired for their personality and for how well they relate to the interviewer on a personal level. "Chemistry" between the candidate and the interviewer, more than qualifications, determines whether the candidate is hired. Interviewing well is usually nothing more than being yourself – your most enthusiastic, most energetic, most engaging self – as well as being a real person.

Train yourself to be real, but not "slick" or "smooth"; to be confident, not cocky; to be prepared, not perfect; and to be conversational, not chatty. Interviewers need to hear about your achievements and accomplishments, but those achievements and accomplishments must be described in a non-arrogant manner. Learn how to "humbly brag." Most importantly, interviewers want to determine how well you will fit into the company's culture and how you will relate to its employees.

Most everything you need for performing well in a job interview is covered in our interviewing principles section (Appendix A). Accordingly, avoid doing or saying anything in an interview that is not covered in that section. Answers to questions noted in that section should be practiced until they are delivered confidently, but don't sound "canned." You should rehearse the "Interview Closing Sequence," the only script which really needs mastering, because setting up the next interview while still in the first interview is the most important step of all. The following illustration presents the "Interview Closing Sequence" which takes place at the end of the interview.

The End of the Interview: The "Interview Closing Sequence"

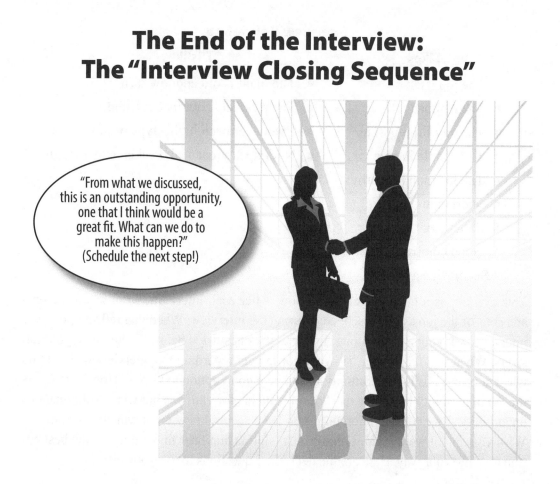

Debrief After Each Interview

Within 10 minutes after leaving an interview, you should sit down in a quiet place, gather your thoughts, and perform within your mind an "interview debrief." Immediately reviewing the interview is critical to the job search process because your memory is fresh; as each hour goes by, you will begin to forget the details of your meetings. Also, some things that were said in the interview which seemed insignificant to you at the time they were spoken may, upon reflection, become significant.

Write down as much as possible of what you can remember. These notes will serve you well in your preparation for subsequent interviews with this company. The notes will also help you compose the thank-you notes you need to write as soon as you complete your debrief. (Of course, if you know for certain that you have no interest in moving to a next step, the debriefing process is not necessary.)

A good method for conducting your debrief is to ask yourself a series of questions relating to what you liked, and did not like, about the interview. Here is an example of the possible pros and cons identified by a candidate who has just completed a job interview:

Interview Debriefing

Likes	Dislikes
▪ The job itself	▪ The plant is old and low tech
▪ The company	▪ The product is not that exciting
▪ The guy I'd report to	▪ I've never been in this type of job before
▪ The people in general	▪ Nothing is a real deal breaker here, though
▪ The location is nearby	
▪ Short commute	
▪ Should pay well	
▪ Good company benefits	
▪ Seems like a good fit	

This example is a good exercise to follow. After each interview, write down the pros and cons of the job as you discovered during the interview. When you reflect upon your interview, ask yourself questions similar to the ones listed below. Write down your answers. When you finish your list, your gut feeling regarding the interview will tell you whether or not this job opportunity would be a good option to pursue. However, unless the job opportunity had some real "deal breakers" for you, it is not wise to eliminate an opportunity from consideration until you have secured new employment for yourself. What you do not want to do is eliminate an option and later find out it was the best option to come your way. Here are the debriefing questions to ask yourself:

- How do I think the interview went, overall?
- How was the personal chemistry between myself and the interviewer(s)?
- What do they want someone to do in the position? Can I do it?
- How long was I there?
- Who else did I meet?
- Who else do I need to meet in order to receive an offer?
- Did they ask me about money?
- What did I like about the opportunity?
- What are things I did not like, or concerns I may have?
- Do I see myself doing this job?
- When is my next interview scheduled with them?
- How would I rank this opportunity against the others I've interviewed for?
- Do I want the job?
- Of the concerns I listed, how would I rank them in order of importance?

The last question about "concerns" needs special attention. Ironically, the concerns you ranked last, or least important to you, are probably the biggest ones for you. When listing employment concerns, many people list the main issues for them last, and they often do this subconsciously, or they are embarrassed to admit a concern because of its nature. For example, many military officers leave the service because they are tired of leading large groups. They prefer to work in small groups, or even solo. However, they rarely will admit that in interviews, because it's considered highly unprofessional within the military for an officer not to have a strong desire to lead. When these officers interview for positions which require leadership, in order to not appear unprofessional, they will often give reasons for not accepting a position which have nothing to do with leading people.

Send Thank-You Notes

Be sure to immediately write thank-you notes after each interview. These should be addressed to the person who interviewed you as well as to every important person you met at the company, which includes support staff and secretaries. The notes should be composed within one hour after leaving the interview and emailed to each recipient at the company. Make sure you include proper titles, spelling, and grammar, and add things which can give each note greater impact.

Some job search experts do not recommend emailing a thank-you note because doing so implies laziness and informality. If you follow that advice, you'll waste a golden opportunity to influence a company's decision. Emailing thank-you notes implies action orientation, speed, and technical savvy – what business is all about. Also, each of the notes should include something unique about each recipient, and not be the same wording for all. That alone has a very positive impact on the recipients.

> *Address your thank-you notes to the interviewer as well as other important people you meet at the company.*

The real purpose of thank-you notes for the 30/30 program is not to say "thank you" but to influence the decision of each person who met you, and to do that **before** the interviewers meet to discuss you. Sending notes through regular mail (snail mail) may result in lost opportunities – by the time your mailed notes are received, the decision about you may have already been made. Let others say "thank you" through the post office…while you get the job! Here's an example of an email "thank-you" note:

Dear Mr. [Name]:

It was a pleasure meeting you today! I cannot express to you enough my appreciation for lining up your team members on such short notice to meet with me. I am very impressed with everything and everyone at XYZ Company. I think it would be a great fit, and I am confident I could do a great job for you as a warehouse manager. I have done it before, and I am excited about doing it again for you.

I look forward to returning to the plant on Tuesday, [date], to continue our discussions.

Thanks again, have a great weekend, and have fun fishing offshore!

Sincerely,

Bill Smith

Contact Good References

Once you have had your first face-to-face interview with an employer, you should telephone your references and let them know they may be contacted soon by either the employer himself/herself, or by someone else at the compa-
ny he/she is from. **Never** allow a reference to be caught
by surprise. Your references should be former direct
supervisors, not friends or family members. If you are
transitioning military, you should provide the employer
with copies of performance evaluations (called "fitness
reports" in the Navy, Marine Corps, and Coast Guard,
and "Evaluation Reports" or "OERs" in the Army and
Air Force). Some companies may actually wish to call
former military superiors, but they will usually rely upon military performance evaluations alone as sufficient because military people are difficult to locate.

> *Ensure that your references are reachable whenever possible, and prepared to say good things about you.*

The key regarding references is to ensure that your references are reachable whenever possible, and prepared to say good things about you. Many would ask "Isn't
that unethical to ensure they are going to say good things?" No, it isn't, it's **smart**.
When you contact a reference, you should say the following in a voicemail, email,
or in person:

[Name]:

*I'm in the middle of a job search and just had a great meeting with [name of employer]
of [company]. He's discussing with me the possibility of my joining his organization
and much of whether or not that happens will be determined by the references he
receives from people I have worked for. He may be calling you, and I hope I can count
on your help in landing this great opportunity. I really appreciate anything you can
do, and please call me if I can provide any information for you. Thanks.*

[your name]

While this message does not say anything unethical, it makes it clear that much rides on
the reference provided by the recipient of the message; i.e., a bad reference will sink the
candidate's chances for this opportunity. Often in cases where a reference's opinion of
a person is not good, the reference will say he cannot give a reference because of company policy or, at worst, he gives a "faint praise" reference that neither enthusiastically
endorses nor harms the candidate. We learned through experdsience that only the most
results-oriented, business-minded, and courageous people will give an outright negative
reference, even if warranted. That's because in this age of litigation, most people will
play it safe and give a neutral rather than negative reference, and (hopefully) not need
to defend themselves in lawsuits.

Close Effectively

Closing should be a continuous process in job hunting. In a business context, the term "closing" comes from the sales world and means obtaining decisions, whether good news or bad. All interviews are "selling situations" and, as such, you should have a goal for every interview you go on. Your goal in interviewing is to acquire one of only three acceptable outcomes from each interview.

The only acceptable outcomes – either positive and negative – from your job interview should be:

1. A decision for a second interview with day and time on the calendar
2. A decision for an offer of employment with salary specified
3. A decision for terminating the screening process – there is no "fit"

Learn to go into all interviews determined to come out with one of these three outcomes or decisions. Avoid settling for *"I will get back to you"* as an outcome. *"I will get back to you"* is how almost all interviewers conclude interviews, even when they have high interest in the candidate. Our 30/30 program shows you how to answer that most common (yet unacceptable) ending and convert it into one of the three acceptable outcomes listed above, and to do so without sounding pushy, aggressive, or desperate. That is accomplished by properly closing your interviews.

Why is *"I will get back to you"* at the conclusion of an interview unacceptable? It's unacceptable because, by settling for that outcome, you are opening the door to the passage of time, and the passage of time kills hires. That's because an interviewer's interest in you will never be greater than during the time you are actually sitting in front of him/her. Even if an interviewer is strongly interested in you, each day that passes after meeting you will cause the interviewer's interest to wane, eventually to the point where you are no longer considered a high priority, and that applies no matter how well the interview went. Also, would you prefer to know the day of an interview that the interviewer has decided not to move forward, or would you rather wait to learn that fact a week or two later? You need to learn to get decisions from interviewers in order to close effectively.

> *An interviewer's interest in you will never be greater than when you are actually sitting in front of him/her.*

How is closing performed without sounding pushy, aggressive, or desperate? We detail this closing process in our discussion of interviewing principles in Appendix A. For now, know that closing in interviews is mostly a function of simply asking the interviewer at the end of the interview to set up a second meeting. Most interviewers will give a straight answer if they don't want to do that because they do not want to hire you. Unfortunately, rarely are they asked because most candidates do not want to learn the truth if they are not being considered further. Or, they do not ask because they do not truly believe that by the end of a first interview, the interviewer has decided whether or not to move to the next step.

By the time an interview is ending, barring an unforeseen interruption which terminates the interview prematurely, the interviewer has decided whether or not to move to the next step with you. Interviewing is almost exactly the same as dating, and that's because hiring is a big emotional commitment for a hiring manager, just as dating someone is also an emotional commitment. Employers do not hire "maybes," just as intelligent people never marry "maybes." Almost all daters know by the conclusion of a first date whether or not they want to date someone a second time, and almost all interviewers know by the end of a first interview whether or not to proceed with a candidate. Learn to ask interviewers whether or not they desire to go to the next step with you. Study and master the Interview Closing Sequence in Appendix A (page 89).

Negotiate Offers

You don't need to be a skilled negotiator to negotiate employment offers – only a **competent negotiator**. Such a negotiator is someone who knows how to get an employer to his best offer without irritating the employer. Negotiating employment offers is fraught with peril, yet too many employment advisors fail to emphasize that fact. It is perilous because when you attempt to negotiate changes to an offer, you must be willing to risk losing that opportunity altogether. That's because until an employment offer is accepted, it can be rescinded at any time.

Some employment experts perpetuate myths about negotiating employment offers that cost job hunters opportunities. The three most common negotiation myths include:

1. **Employers will try to acquire your talents at the lowest compensation possible.** Employers aren't stupid. After all, what employer wants to hire you and then have you become angry or possibly even quit the company when you learn you were "low-balled"? Salary information frequently leaks out to the displeasure of fellow employees. In reality, most companies make fair, reasonable, and often generous offers because they want employees to come aboard motivated, and to remain so. They also need to maintain competitive compensation for their industry or they will lose people.

2. **Rarely is a company's first offer its best offer.** This is a very damaging myth which is sometimes true, but rarely. More often than not, except in cases of high-level executive hires, a company's first offer is its best offer. If you are a middle manager or lower, it is never wise to ask for changes to an offer you can live with, especially if it is with a company located where you want to be. In Neil's 25 years in placement, he has frequently seen someone make the mistake of asking for more compensation and then have their original offer rescinded because the employer felt the candidate would not be satisfied with what he could offer.

3. **Companies respect good negotiators. They expect you to negotiate when they make you an offer, and will think less of you if you do not negotiate.** Forget the popular notion that everything is negotiable. In fact, few people are more annoying to employers than so-called good negotiators. How many times

have you tried to sell something and encountered someone who thought he was a clever negotiator? In negotiating employment offers, you are risking angering your future boss (and/or losing the offer) each time you ask for a change to the original offer. And even if you manage to negotiate some nice additions to your package, you will probably arrive on your new job with a new boss who is already a bit irritated with you because you were not satisfied with his original offer – something he felt was fair and reasonable.

Our best advice is this: if an opportunity is located where you want it to be located, and the offer satisfies your "must haves" and many of your "nice to haves," do not risk losing the opportunity by attempting to change your offer. If you must ask for changes, pick the most important one, and do not **ever** ask for more than two changes.

Get Hired

You are considered to be hired when you receive three verbal commitments:

1. an offer
2. your acceptance
3. a start date

These verbal commitments are usually followed up in writing. If any one of these three elements is lacking, you do not have a secured position with a company.

Most companies will extend employment offers verbally and wait for a verbal acceptance before writing up a formal offer letter. That's because no company wants to ask an employee to take the time to draft a formal letter if it is uncertain whether or not the candidate will be accepting the offer. For this reason, **never** tell a prospective employer that you would like to see everything in writing before making any decisions. That will be interpreted negatively by the company and could even be interpreted as distrust, something which could easily cause the company to reconsider hiring you. In fact, in the search and placement industry, we know that whenever a candidate tells us that he/she needs to see an offer in writing before making a decision, that means the candidate is not going to accept an offer from the company. It's a stall tactic used by candidates to avoid making a commitment. For that reason, smart placement professionals never "extend" an offer; they only "confirm" a placement. They accomplish that by gaining a commitment from the candidate to accept an offer before going to the company to ask for the offer on the candidate's behalf.

Resignation, Counteroffers, and Continuing Actions

Once your hiring is firmed up (i.e., you have received an offer of employment, have given your acceptance, and you have a start date), you will need to resign from your present employment (if you are employed) and then proceed through the interim period prior to reporting to your new position. That means the most emotionally difficult period for you is about to begin. Your initial happiness at landing new employment may be followed by a period of self doubt, second-guessing your decision, and possibly anxiety.

Take comfort in knowing these emotions are normal and almost always subside as soon as you are in your new job. See our resignation tips in Appendix C (pages 113-118).

Changing employers is an extremely stressful undertaking for any person and his or her family. It has often been compared to the stress level experienced by a death in the family or divorce. Additionally, if you are relocating, the stress level will be even higher, even if you have had a strong and lasting desire to get to where you are moving to. Because of the level of stress, you will need coping strategies against that stress for your peace of mind. The greatest level of stress comes from what is commonly referred to as "buyer's remorse." Buyer's remorse is a natural response people have whenever they are making a big venture into the unknown. It is characterized by a continuous self-questioning of the decision to take the new job. That is one big reason why, if you

> *Changing employers can be very stressful – comparable to a death in the family or a divorce. It also may involve "buyer's remorse."*

are presently employed, you should not give more than two weeks notice. The longer you remain in your present company after resigning, the greater the self doubt and buyer's remorse become.

Your best defense against the stress of job change and/or relocation is to know what to expect, and to be prepared for what actions to take and when to take them. The interview principles outlined in Appendix A are a good guide for dealing with the stress and tasks associated with job change. It also will help you deal with your present employer if he/she attempts to "counteroffer" you or persuade you to remain with your present company. You and your family should review these principles and then discuss it together.

There are continuous actions that you should take after you have accepted an offer of employment and prior to reporting for work. Most significantly, you will need to ensure that all pre-employment tasks are completed, such as a physical examination or background check. Make certain your credit score and driving record are accurate and that there is no inaccurate information on the Internet about you (or someone with the same name), which can sink your new job before you arrive there. If there is someone with the same name on the Internet and questionable material related to that person, make certain to alert your new company to that fact. (Example: there is another Neil McNulty who has a very "edgy" website, something out of character for this author.) Regularly check the Internet, always looking for information that could possibly harm your profile. Since employers search the Internet for information about new hires, make sure the information about you is accurate and not about someone else.

The goal is to arrive in your new job with a fresh, new, and exciting beginning!

Appendix A

Interviewing Principles You Should Never Forget

"The interview is the single most important step to getting a job offer. Perform well and you'll get the job!"

T HOROUGH PREPARATION IS essential for doing well in a job interview. Indeed, this is not the time to appear authentic and spontaneous by just "being yourself" or "winging it." Employers expect to see your **best self** – both verbal and nonverbal – on display during a job interview. Unfortunately, many talented candidates miss some great opportunities, because they fail to sufficiently prepare for an interview. That one unexpected question, that one awkward moment, the "off-target" answer – and the opportunity is lost. Often, it's lost due to mishandling a question or situation or because of overconfidence.

Interviews Are Often a One-Way Street

Confidence is a good thing in interviewing; overconfidence is not. Since interviewing is something we all do so infrequently in our careers, anything other than an attitude of "I need to work hard for this upcoming interview" is overconfidence. Too many candidates approach interviews with this attitude: "I always do well on interviews, and besides, I have a lot to offer a company. I'm interviewing them as much as they're interviewing me. After all, interviewing is a two-way street." Indeed, many believe the interview is just another two-way conversation to exchange ideas and learn more about each other. Not surprisingly, they prepare accordingly, which means little preparation for this important "conversation."

"Two-way street" thinking is favored by too many so-called "experts" who often miss this important point:

> Unless you have an extremely rare and special skill, you are famous, or you are interviewing in your father's company, interviewing should primarily be a one-way street where your job is to **sell an organization on why it should hire you.**

The two-way street begins when you begin asking questions about the organization and when the organization starts negotiating with you. This observation may be unsettling for many people, especially those who have accomplished much, have great careers going, are justifiably proud of their accomplishments, and believe that companies should be pursuing them, not the other way around. Unfortunately, such people tend not to receive job offers until they change their approach and do the types of things described in this appendix. That's because no matter how outstanding someone may be, a smart organization will not hire someone unless it clearly sees how that person will **add value** to the organization. Therefore, it's extremely important that you market yourself correctly to potential employers, and especially during the critical job interview(s).

> *A smart organization will not hire someone unless it clearly sees how that person will **add value** to the organization.*

Whatever your career, you've mastered it because of your many **accomplishments**. And that's exactly what you want to communicate to potential employers who are looking for exceptional talent – you're a successful person who will **repeat your pattern of accomplishments** in another employment setting.

Inside Secrets of Placement Experts

In the remaining pages of this appendix, we reveal **insider interview tips** based on years of placement experience. This experience involves thousands of interviews between candidates and employers, at all levels, and on detailed questioning of both employers and candidates after each interview.

Unlike many job search experts who come from other professional fields, our expertise is based on nuts-and-bolts experiences in the **placement field**. We're literally in the job search trenches on a day-to-day basis with hundreds and thousands of people and jobs. We focus on working closely with both candidates and employers in the process of repeatedly finding and filling jobs. We actually engage in job hunting for a living and participate in the hiring processes of hundreds of different companies, and from both sides (candidate and company). At the same time, which may be unfortunate for most job seekers, we are also the least likely to share our techniques and information with someone unless that person is one of our candidates for placement or for one of our 30/30 programs, such as this one. Like magicians, the most successful placement professionals are not going to reveal secrets through job hunting books. However, we're going to do it anyway, and you'll be one of the beneficiaries of our many insider secrets!

As you get ready to go on job interviews, you should primarily focus on the information given in the following pages. Here we cover everything you need to know and master for interviewing success. However, you **must** follow our advice closely in order to make it work to your advantage, even though at times it may seem counter-intuitive. Please study, learn, and internalize **everything** on the following pages.

12 Key Interview Principles

Let's talk about principles rather than laws when it comes to the job interview. As you'll quickly see once you start interviewing, several fundamental principles or "rules of thumb" govern interviewing with an iron fist. These are not laws because exceptions to them do occur. Nonetheless, these are the most important interviewing principles that should guide you in preparing for and succeeding in the job interview. Some principles you may have heard before, some not. Learn them all, and believe them, because all of them are more or less true and effective!

1. **First impressions have a greater impact on job interviewing than almost any other interpersonal activity.** You've heard it said many times that you have only one chance to make a first impression, whether meeting someone for the first time in a business or social situation. This is especially true for job interviewing. Indeed, one of the fundamental purposes of an initial interview, from the employer's perspective, is to conclude that first interview only after a positive or negative opinion of the candidate has been formed, and that opinion will be unchangeable. You can believe this because it's always true, even if an interviewer denies making such ostensibly snap decisions.

   How do we know this with such certainty? Because Neil has debriefed thousands of candidates who have gone through first-time interviews. He quickly learned that employers/interviewers never bring someone back for a second interview unless their impression from the first interview was not just positive, but highly positive. Whenever an interviewer's feedback was "I don't want to rule this person out. I'm on the fence about him or her so let me think this one over," Neil found that not a single one of those candidates was offered the job. The lesson here is this: when an employer is shaking your hand at the end of the first interview (barring an interruption which ends the interview prematurely), the interviewer has decided whether or not to bring you back for another interview. Believe it...it is **always true** based on our experience! Accordingly, you better **spark** from the moment you meet the interviewer until you close and part ways.

   > *It's really true – you never have a second chance to make a good first impression. So you better get it right from the start!*

   For this reason, you **must** master the interview technique of directly asking an interviewer at the end of an interview if you "fit" what he or she is looking for, as part of the "Interview Closing Sequence" you will learn later in this section.

   Perhaps you've also heard that an interviewer decides in the first 10 minutes of an interview whether or not to hire the person being interviewed. This is sometimes true, but rarely. What is always true in the first 10 minutes of an interview is the interviewer is deciding whether to spend a full hour with the candidate or to give a shortened **courtesy interview**. "Time is money" applies here.

   You will know a "courtesy interview" when you see it. Courtesy interviews usually last 30 minutes or less in duration and the interviewer asks very few questions because he or she has already ruled you out for whatever reason. The only way to possibly recover your candidacy under such circumstances is to be bold and "go for broke" by stating something like this:

> *"Correct me if I am wrong, but I sense that you do not see me as a good fit for what you're looking for. Let's discuss that and see if it can be overcome. If it can't, that's okay, but what is your area of concern?"*

Under such circumstances, you have only about a 30-percent chance of being considered further because, as mentioned above, the interviewer must have a highly positive first impression of you to move forward. But you have a zero chance without addressing any concern head on. You have nothing to lose by taking this approach. In fact, Neil has debriefed employers who were turned around positively by such a confident and perceptive candidate. If your instincts are telling you that the interviewer is not totally enamored with you, then you're probably correct. Ask what the concern is!

Due to the critical nature of the first 10 minutes of an interview, you must also be thoroughly prepared for tough questions from the moment you walk into the interviewer's office. Thorough preparation is the vital key to smoothly moving through the early minutes of an interview.

Never give details on any specific area of your background until you know for certain it is what the interviewer wants.

Always give the interviewer a deep, firm handshake, but not a bone crusher, and smile. Sometimes an interviewer will accidentally (or purposefully) give you a handful of fingers, i.e., a "mushy" handshake. When this occurs, smile and do the handshake over again with the statement "I blew that one...I know how important it is that I give you my regular, firm handshake!" It is far better to do this than to let it be and then have the interviewer think you have a lousy handshake.

Learn the most effective way (there is no "best" way, contrary to what the "experts" may say) to handle the "tell me about yourself" question, which is often the first question interviewers ask, simply to break the ice. The effective way to handle the question is to give a two-minute chronological career summary of where you were and what your positions were. Give no detailed information, no personal information, and do not rush or ramble, and do not pause. The last two sentences of your two-minute summary should be:

> *"This brings me to today. What are some of the duties and responsibilities of the position?"* or *"What are some of the needs that you have, or problems you'd like someone to solve for your company?"*

You must say the above because you want to **understand the need to be satisfied** before getting into details of your background. **Listen** to the employer and tailor your answers to only those things he or she said were important.

In the first few minutes of an interview, you should have a general idea of what the company is looking for if you did your homework, so your two-minute summary should be tailored as best you can to what you know of the interviewer's needs. But you could be wrong, and he could also be thinking of creating an entirely new position. Additionally, sometimes a hiring authority will change his or her mind about the parameters of a position just before or even during your interview. For this reason, **always listen** to the interviewer for **cues** as to what he or she wants to hear and carefully watch what you say during the interview. A good rule to follow is this: Never give details on any specific area of your background until you know for certain it is what the interviewer wants, and that is when you know it will solve a problem or satisfy a need for the interviewer and his company.

2. **Employers hire candidates who show early on that they want to work for their company.**
   This is the old principle of mutual attraction between strangers – people tend to like people who like them! You do this by showing desire and enthusiasm the moment you arrive at the job interview. Call it your "spark" or "glow." Being "low-keyed," "laid back," or "cool" won't get you very far with a prospective employer. Always go to all interviews, including the first interview with a company, as though you want to work for the company, even when you aren't sure. While you should not go overboard, be blindly foolish, or appear overly eager or desperate for the job, don't be cautious, reserved or think that playing hard to get will make you more desirable. Never say or display an attitude of "I am willing to hear what they have to say" or "I'm open to checking this out." You won't get to a second interview unless you have an extremely rare or exotic skill which the company must acquire despite your apparent lackluster personality and drive. Companies want to see **desire** from the beginning in candidates they invite back or make offers to because they don't want to be turned down. Open-mindedness doesn't get you job offers. Desire does.

> *Go into every interview as if you want the job. To do any-thing less is to unknowingly disqualify yourself from further consideration.*

   On the first interview with a company, you really don't know whether the opportunity is the right one for you, so your desire is really an act at first. However, it could be the right place for you once you have more information, even if you didn't think so before the interview. Act from the start as though it's the right place because the first people who interview you at that company will reject you if you don't show a lot of interest and enthusiasm for their company from the start. Many times Neil debriefed someone who went into an interview cautiously and reserved (though they thought they were enthusiastic) because they weren't sure it would be a good fit. A typical summary debriefing observation is this:

> *"At first I was a little bit cautious, because I really wasn't sure this was right for me, but it turned out to be okay."*

These words describe a situation that went nowhere. It could have turned out incredibly well if the candidate had followed our simple rule of **expressing desire and enthusiasm** throughout the interview. Sadly, these people are always rejected by the company because the first people who met them, prior to the candidate's realization of how great an opportunity was in front of them, saw and reported a reserved demeanor, no "spark," no "fire in the belly," no desire and enthusiasm for the company, and, accordingly, graded them low on interpersonal skills or some other "chemistry-related" trait.

Again, no matter how outstanding your background and qualifications are, you will be rejected if you do not show enthusiasm for the organization and position from the outset.

Go into every interview as if you want the job, even if you have doubts, and on your drive home decide whether the opportunity is really the right one for you. To do anything less than this is to unknowingly disqualify yourself from further consideration. They simply won't want you back for a second interview since there may be more desirable fish in the hiring pond!

3. Interviewing ability is what lands the job – not credentials.

Most hiring authorities do not enjoy interviewing. Unless you are interviewing with a Human Resources recruiter, you are most likely interviewing with someone who would prefer to be doing his or her regular job. (And most Human Resources recruiters dislike interviewing also!) There are two basic types of interviewers at a company: prepared and unprepared. Fortunately for candidates, it is the exception when an interviewer is prepared. Accordingly, we have found that many interviewers are poorly skilled and simply "wing" their way from one question to the next, or don't ask any questions at all! A few interviewers plan their questions, but most do not. The worst interviewers simply fill the time with a description of the company and position, ask a few basic questions, and then complain afterward that the candidate "didn't have the necessary experience."

It's how well one relates personally to the interviewer and how one fits the company culture – not qualifications – that clinches the job offer.

Because of a lack of interviewing skills (though they would never admit that), most hiring managers rely upon personal chemistry or "gut feel" – not qualifications – as the main determining factor for selecting the person they are going to hire. One must certainly demonstrate that he or she is capable of doing the job, but it's how well one relates personally to the interviewer and how one fits the company culture that clinches the job offer. Hiring is a very important "buying decision" for a manager, similar to the purchase of a home or other large investment where the stakes are high. As with all important buying decisions, once all the information and facts are evaluated, emotions and instincts play a large role in making the final decision. Accordingly, a job candidate **must** learn everything possible about the person the position reports to, the company, corporate culture, position responsibilities, and people he or she will be meeting during the interview process. Dig deep into the Internet and find out if the interviewer has given any speeches, published any books or articles, or has other noteworthy achievements, and mention them (favorably, of course!) at key moments in the interview. (This technique has a very positive effect on an interviewer, especially if he or she has written a book and the candidate has read it.)

A candidate should also practice the skill of diplomatically taking over the direction of an interview if it is obviously going poorly due to the employer's lack of interviewing skills. Say positive, original things in the interview which other candidates are not saying, and stand out in a positive way by separating yourself from the other candidates. Accomplishing these things takes practice!

4. **Unless it is an accounting, scientific, or research position, most companies want extroverted, outgoing people.**
This may seem obvious, but companies tend to hire people who know how to carry on a conversation with a stranger, people who show some spark, people who smile a lot and are very personable. Unless the position was for a highly technical or accounting position, almost all of Neil's placements have been people who were outgoing, friendly, and engaging by nature. If they were introverts by nature, he trained them to perform in an extroverted manner for the interviews he sent them on. Why? Because in his experience, people who act introverted and analytical during interviews tend not to receive job offers. The reason isn't because there is anything wrong with introverts. Rather, it is because introverts tend to do a poor job of describing their achievements and accomplishments in a way that will "light a fire" inside an interviewer. Also, many interviewers want to be "entertained" by candidates.

When an interviewer is looking for someone to hire, it's as if he or she is acting as a casting director for a key role in the director's most important production ever: his business. As with the performing arts, the person who wins the role is going to be the one who clearly stands out without overdoing it; the one who "wows" the interviewer. That means saying and doing things other candidates are not saying and doing. If that's not your style, then work at altering your style for interviews. To do that requires rehearsal and practice, but it can be done.

Learn to articulate your achievements and accomplishments by practicing, and don't be shy. Remember, if the interviewer is not prepared, as many aren't, it will be to your benefit to be able to steer the interview in directions which accent your strongest skills and attributes. If you know you are introverted by nature, you can overcome that through preparation. Be conversational when answering questions. Do not give "yes" or "no" answers. However, be aware of the difference between being conversational and talking too much. People who clam up or simply sit there and await the next question during interviews are indicating to the interviewer that they lack confidence, have something to hide, or are simply boring, none of which may be true.

A very effective technique for answering questions relating to your accomplishments is to tell a "mini-story" about each. These are "two-minute anecdotes" using the SOAR approach to storytelling: Situation, Objective, Action my team took under my leadership, Results achieved. Prepare three "SOAR" mini-stories before each interview.

Listen when the interviewer is speaking, and don't **ever** argue or interrupt. However, do not allow the interviewer to go off on tangents or to spend a lot of time not discussing how you would fit the position and company.

Finally, Neil has had introverted people tell him that they felt it was "deceptive" to act in a manner that is not "natural" for them. That is a flawed rationalization and a recipe for continuous interview failure. Nobody is his or her "natural" self in an interview, because interviewing isn't a natural situation! People should be their **best selves** in an interview, or they shouldn't be interviewing. All employers know you're on your best behavior during an interview, so it is not deceptive to be better than your usual self at such times.

> *Immediately write thank-you notes after a job interview – within an hour, not 24 hours.*

Communication also means written material. Immediately after an interview, always write a thank-you note to each person you met, including support staff and secretaries, and write them the same day of the interview, preferably within one half hour of leaving the building. While you also may want to follow up by sending a thank-you note by regular mail, always immediately send one by email.

Taking immediate action is the key to sending effective thank-you notes. Such behavior will make a very favorable impression on the readers who will see you as being an action-oriented person. They also will see you as someone who is people-oriented, because you sent thank-you notes to lower-echelon people such as support staff.

Do not fail to take immediate action here! This is a critical time which could pay big dividends…or ruin your chances by failing to act promptly.

Keep each note short and to the point, perhaps eight to ten lines maximum. Do not go into detail on anything because you could write something which accidentally damages your candidacy. Furthermore, do not make each note exactly the same. Show each interviewer that you remember him or her specifically by writing a line or two regarding something they mentioned, perhaps something relating to sports or hobbies. Make certain spelling, punctuation, titles, and grammar are correct. Avoid overused phrases such as "thank you for taking time out from your busy schedule…"

Neil once had two candidates who were tied for a position and the offer went to the candidate who wrote individual thank-you notes to each of eight people who met him, including the reception area attendant. In each note he recalled something unique about the reader. You can bet these people were impressed! The hiring manager told Neil that the extra effort and attention to detail made the difference.

Surprisingly, despite the importance of timely thank-you notes, about half of the people who read this book will wait too long to write them (more than 24 hours after the interview, which puts them in the same class as the other candidates) or not write them at all. This is due mostly to laziness, or a feeling that things went so well that to get the offer a note won't be necessary. Be warned: Neil has met and/or spoken with many employers who will not hire someone they otherwise would have hired if they do not send a prompt thank-you note! Many employers regard sending thank-you notes as common courtesy, but also as a sound business practice. In fact, they view the notes as one indication of the way you would deal with customers and co-workers. Writing such notes is an **act of thoughtfulness** – a value highly prized by employers who take such social graces with strangers seriously.

Don't lose out on an opportunity because of such a preventable error!

5. Most interviewers ask the same questions.
Most interviewers tend to cover the same things in an interview. Rarely do they ask really tough or unusual questions. This is normally due to the lack of preparation mentioned above. However, even when prepared, interviewers tend to ask the same types of questions. For the most part, they tend to cover four basic areas, so be prepared for and practice answers to each of these types of questions:

- icebreaker questions
- skills and qualifications questions
- corporate personality questions
- personal chemistry questions

There are other areas which may be covered that fall outside of these four categories, but these four areas are the most frequently covered.

Icebreaker questions are asked in the first ten minutes and are designed to ease the initial nervousness and awkwardness for the candidate (and for the interviewer!) These will be small-talk questions about the weather, news, etc.

The **skills and qualifications questions** are usually asked next. These are used to determine whether the candidate can actually do the job. This is where the interviewer decides whether to spend a full hour or have a shortened "courtesy" interview with the candidate. The questions will focus on a candidate's specific experience and qualifications as they relate to the position to be filled.

Corporate personality questions are used to determine whether the candidate will fit the culture at the company.

Personal chemistry questions are used to determine whether the actual hiring manager will enjoy having this person on his or her team.

Make no mistake here: the most important questions are the personal chemistry and corporate personality questions. However, make sure that you demonstrate clearly to the interviewer that you can actually do the job and do it well.

6. Murphy's Law is everywhere in interviews.

Murphy's Law is the famous old adage that seems to frequently affect lives: "Anything that can go wrong will go wrong." Even though most interviews follow a predictable format, it doesn't mean that everything will run smoothly. In fact, a great number of interviews Neil has conducted, arranged, debriefed, or simply heard about had some type of problem. This is especially true for travel interviews. Airline delays, rental car snafus, hotel reservations which disappear at the front desk at midnight, lost luggage, etc., all tend to happen during travel for interviews.

Even during interviews calamities can happen. For example, you go out for a meal with the interviewer, and the waitress spills coffee on you. You arrive at the interview on time, only to discover that the interviewer is going to be an hour late. Someone dents your rental car which you parked in the company lot. Hopefully you're covered by insurance, but maybe not.

Because of the pervasive nature of Murphy's Law during interviews, it is imperative that a candidate be flexible, resilient, and retain a sense of humor in the face of disaster. How you handle the unexpected frustrations during interviews can work tremendously to your advantage (or to your detriment). Neil once had a candidate take two days to get to an interview because of airline weather delays. He arrived completely exhausted, frustrated, fed up, and without luggage. But he kept his sense of humor. Upon arrival, he told his interviewer that if anyone had "earned the job," he had, and "big time." Who else had slept the previous two nights on an airport lounge seat, eaten unappetizing airline terminal food, or gone without a toothbrush, comb, soap, or shower for two days? He got the job not only because he could do the job and was an excellent candidate, but mostly because he never lost his sense of humor in the face of such frustrating challenges.

Always expect and allow time for travel delays, and call if you are going to be late. If possible, speak with the interviewer. But if you must leave a message, leave it on the interviewer's voicemail or send an email (if you have the address). Don't leave your only message with an assistant, who might forget to deliver the message, and the interviewer would then believe you stood him up!

7. **Your only goals for the first interview should be to receive either a job offer or an invitation to a second interview.**

The moment you leave an interview, the interviewer begins to lose interest in you, no matter how well the interview went. Although you received "in the moment" attention that may have felt good, that doesn't mean such attention will continue strong for very long and will result in more interviews and eventually a job offer. Here's what happens: The interviewer goes back to his normal daily routine and begins to forget about you thanks to the demands of his or her own job and other distractions that increasingly put a fog around you. As the fog gets thicker, you may disappear altogether. The fog usually comes in like this: At first, an interviewer forgets only the details about you. After about five days, the

> *The moment you leave an interview, the interviewer begins to lose interest as the fog of daily routines clouds his memory of you.*

interviewer will remember only your most significant characteristics, no matter how outstanding you were in the meeting. After 10 days, an interviewer will have difficulty remembering what you look like and will begin to rely solely on your resume – not what you said in your interview – as the basis for considering you further. For these reasons, it is imperative that you master what we call the **Interview Closing Sequence**.

The Interview Closing Sequence is a highly effective scheduling technique for use at the conclusion of an interview. It consists of two simple parts:

1. Summary
2. Close

In the **summary**, the candidate looks for cues that the interview is about to end. This could be the interviewer looking at his watch, or telling someone on the telephone that he will call back in a few minutes, or something similar. (You will know when it's ending.) When this occurs, it is your cue to quickly summarize your achievements, accomplishments, and personality, and emphasize how all three would fit well in the job.

Then you should ask the following question, and ask it with these exact words:

> *"Mr. or Ms. Interviewer [give name], from what we've discussed today, this seems like an outstanding company and opportunity, one I would definitely want to take to the next step. I realize this is only the first interview, but at this point in the process, do you see me as a potential fit for what you are looking for?"*

This may sound very forward, but it really isn't. Remember, by the time an interviewer begins to close your interview; he or she has already decided whether or not to bring you in for a second interview. If you ask the question confidently, courteously, and in a conversational tone, you will not sound overly forward. It will sound like a natural ending to the interview, and you will probably greatly impress the interviewer with your straightforward businesslike style.

If the interviewer believes you could be a fit, he will tell you so, without hesitation. He will say, "Yes, I do. I think you would fit well." However, if he does not see you as a fit, he will pause, look away, and be noncommittal. One thing is certain: the interviewer had decided whether or not to go to the next step with you before you asked that question, and asking the question will not change that decision to a "no" if the answer is "yes." If the interviewer says you would fit, you respond by saying:

> *"That's great. I would really love to put a second appointment on my calendar. I have a proposal for you. Can we plan on getting together again here at your offices on X date and X time [*make it no more than five days out and at the same time as your present interview*], and if anything changes between now and then, just leave a voicemail message on the number on the resume with the better day and time?"*

More often than not, the interviewer will pull out his calendar and schedule the next appointment right there, without missing a beat. However, unless you ask, the employer will not do it no matter how well the interview went, because he won't think to do it.

If you set up the next appointment, and the interviewer says to call the day before to "confirm" (that's a problem in disguise…if you don't get him on the phone, you won't know for sure if it's on or not, and if you do get him on the phone, his interest will have waned by then due to time passage, or he will have forgotten, and it is then too easy for the employer to make up an excuse to cancel), you should say this:

The passage of time results in a dulling of enthusiasm for the candidate and canceling the interview.

> *"That's fine. If we miss each other, what is your email address?"*

Then you should plan on leaving a voicemail and email the night before (after hours!) saying "looking forward to seeing you again and will be there as planned at X time." Do not give the employer an opportunity to speak with you or contact you prior to the second interview or you run a high risk of his or her canceling.

Here's the bottom line regarding **confirmation calls**: They are actually simply the interviewer's last opportunity to ask "Do I really want to spend more time with this person?" More often than not, the passage of time results in a dulling of enthusiasm for the candidate and canceling the interview.

For sales positions, you are guaranteed NOT to receive a second interview unless you attempt to pin down the next interview during the first. Your sales ability is being evaluated, and a good salesperson always attempts to pin down a second appointment with a prospect.

If the interviewer replies with "Yes, I think you would fit, but I have other candidates to see before selecting the ones to bring back for another interview" (a common and legitimate response), you should reply:

"I understand. When will you be completed with your first round of interviews?"

The interviewer will reply with a date. You respond with:

"I have a proposal for you. For planning purposes, can we plan on my returning here to your office on X date at X time [the DAY AFTER the employer said he or she would complete first-round interviews]? And if you meet someone between now and then who is a better fit, or something comes up, just leave me a voicemail at the number on my resume canceling the meeting."

Another response employers use is this: "I want you to meet (name) and she isn't here right now, and I don't know her schedule." Your response should be:

"I understand. What day does she return?"

The interviewer will say "I'm not sure" or will respond with a date, especially if it is the boss you need to meet. (Everyone knows when the boss is returning!) If he responds with a return date, you answer with:

"I have a proposal for you. For planning purposes, can we plan on my returning here to your office at X date and X time [the DAY AFTER the person returns] and when you speak with him or her, if that's not a convenient date and time, leave a message on my voicemail with the better date and time?"

In all three situations, the phrase **"I have a proposal for you"** is critical because it takes pressure off the interviewer, but at the same time sets up the goal of scheduling a second meeting with the interviewer. Additionally, use the word **"voicemail"** for future communication. Once an employer decides to rule out a candidate, or deliver bad news such as rescheduling an appointment, we have found that most do not want to speak with that candidate again, a sad reality with most interviewers.

Finally, do not attempt to schedule a next step if the interviewer says you do not fit! In that instance, ask what the "concern" is, attempt to address the concern, and then ask again if you "now fit." (Use the word "concern." Using the word "problem" could cause the interviewer to become defensive and make up a fake excuse.) If the interviewer says "Yes, you now fit," return to the scheduling technique above that fits the scenario and try to set up the next appointment. If the interviewer still balks, drop the issue.

While the preceding techniques may appear to be overly aggressive, especially for relatively introverted individuals, nonetheless, they have worked well for hundreds of our clients. Highly effective at scheduling follow-on appointments, these technique have nearly a 70-percent success rate. You **must** practice and rehearse them repeatedly in order to execute them properly. You must also either lose your fear of using them, or use them despite your fear. It cannot be emphasized enough how critical it is for you to schedule a second appointment on your calendar **before** you leave the first interview. The majority of interview situations will go nowhere without a scheduled appointment coming out of the first, no matter how well the interview seems to go. The reason for that is spelled out in the next principle or Rule 8.

8. **The passage of time eliminates potential job offers.**

You've heard the saying "time is on my side," and in many respects it is. Job interviewing isn't one of them, even if you're employed while looking for a new job. In fact, Neil has kept statistics on every placement he has made in his placement career. Of the hundreds of successful placements he made, 86 percent of them occurred within just 17 days from a first interview to job offer. Since most placements required more than one interview, this means that during that 17-day period at least two interviews took place. Only five percent of his placements have required more than three weeks from the initial interview to an offer of employment.

With each day that passes between interviews, five percent of the chance of receiving an offer dies. If 20 days have passed since a first interview with a company and a second interview has not yet been scheduled, the job-offer prospects for that candidate at that company are essentially over, regardless of how well the first interview seemed to go. If 10 days have passed and no second interview has been scheduled, that candidate has only a 50-percent chance of getting a second interview.

The lesson is this: When you're in an interview and you want another interview with the company, set up the next interview before you leave the interview you are in!

Practice and learn the Interview Closing Sequence and second interview scheduling techniques discussed above until you can say them perfectly. "Saying them perfectly" is nothing more than speaking in a conversational tone. Even though our sequence seems aggressive when read, when spoken correctly, it isn't. Another reason you must schedule the next appointment while you are in an interview is the following principle or Rule 9.

9. **Interviewers always delay making decisions.**

Closely tied into the previous principle is the principle that interviewers don't like to make interviewing and hiring decisions and thus will allow candidates to be left hanging. People have a natural aversion to making hiring decisions and will wait until the decisions cannot be put off any longer. Also, unless you make the effort to schedule the next interview, you will not have the next interview scheduled when you are getting into your car, and that applies even if an interviewer is extremely impressed with you. The reason for this is that hiring authorities always wonder if they're making a mistake when it comes to interviewing and hiring decisions. Ironically, if you ask most managers when they want a position filled, the most common answer is "Yesterday!"

Hiring is probably the toughest decision a manager can make, and the consequences of a mismatch, or hiring mistake, are similar to those of a bad marriage. Of all Neil's placements, only a very small number took place without any pushing or prodding on his part or the job candidate's part. Not only are hiring authorities afraid of making a mistake; they also tend to wonder whether someone better suited to the position and company might be just around the next corner.

> **People have a natural aversion to making hiring decisions and will wait until the decisions cannot be put off any longer.**

Because of this common characteristic of hiring managers, it is **imperative** that a job candidate never state nor imply during or after an interview that he or she is under no time pressure for requiring decisions from companies. For example, when an interviewer asks the "time" question, "When do you need a decision from us?" or "What is your timetable?" do not give the following standard answer, which is designed to show courtesy and politeness and appears to indicate that you are not too hard to get:

> *"I am presently in no hurry. Take your time, as I realize how important it is for the company to make the right decision for this position."*

With that response, even if the company thinks you're ideal for the position, you have guaranteed no decision from that company until it is ready, which will probably be a while. Even if the interview went exceptionally well, and you are confident you are the one they want to hire, you have opened the door to the **passage of time**. It's this passage of time, as discussed in the previous principle, that will dull the company's enthusiasm for you. It will most likely cost you the offer. Companies will always find someone else to hire if given enough time to do so. Do not allow them that time! Again, you need to take **purposeful action** that will secure a positive outcome for you.

The most effective answer to the "time" question is this:

> *"This is a superb opportunity, one that I hope is offered to me. Unfortunately for me, though, there are some important decisions I'm going to be required to make in the near future. Is it at all possible for us to complete your hiring process within the next week or so?"*

If the interviewer responds by asking if you have another offer, you should answer with:

> *"I don't want to look as though I'm playing one company off another, because I'm not, and this opportunity is outstanding. I just have some things I need to act upon and was wondering if it is possible to keep things moving here. Could we schedule the next step in this process right now, while we're together?"*

The key to this principle is that the company's interest in you will never be higher than while you are right there in front of them. Once you leave, their interest will begin to wane, so "strike while the iron's hot"! Remember, it's human nature to delay making difficult decisions until they must be made. It is also human nature to desire something more if there is a chance at losing it. Keep the company guessing without being obvious. If you don't have another opportunity, you didn't tell a lie. You simply stated the fact that you have things requiring action. Those "things" include the obvious – you need a job and a paycheck! If the interviewers assume you have another offer, then allow them to have their assumption. Second guessing in this manner works to your advantage.

One final note regarding time: Do not allow an interviewer to confuse time of availability with time for a decision on your candidacy. Let's take an example from our military clients. Often, interviewers will ask transitioning military candidates when they will be available to come to work for their company. The candidates usually answer by saying "My service ends in [x] number of weeks." If you answer that way, many interviewers will assume they have time to keep looking at other candidates before needing to decide on your candidacy, and then the job opportunity dies for you due to the passage of time.

The most effective response is this:

"Although I am separating on [X] date, I am finalizing right now where I will be going to work because of planning for my separation. What can we do to get this done within the next few days?"

Interviewers will make decisions, usually positive ones, if a candidate initiates the proper techniques for requiring decisions. In Neil's years of placement experience, he has found almost without exception that most interviewers want to **delay** making a final decision on a candidate for as long as possible. The more time companies have, the less chance the candidate will receive an offer. Learn to prod employers to action!

10. Always tailor your resume to the opportunity at hand.

This is one of the easiest things to do with computers and technology at our fingertips, but one of the most neglected. Always have your resume on your computer, available at the stroke of a few keys for alterations. Resumes, like a fine suit, should be carefully tailored to the person who will be interviewing you and to the company and position you are interviewing for. Bring several copies of your resume to the interview. It is unimportant to interviewers that your resume be printed on expensive or fine paper.

What **is** important is that the resume contain the "hot buttons" or **key words** the interviewer is looking for regarding the position that needs to be filled. Neil has had many candidates tell him that they think he has taken too many of their "important" achievements off their resumes, such as the Ph.D. in Business for a production manager candidate he once interviewed, or the "marathon runner" he deleted off the resume of another. It is always unethical to put on a resume what you do not have, but never unethical, and necessary, to take off something you have but which **doesn't** enhance your candidacy for the specific company, position, and interviewer you are targeting.

Never put on a resume that you are a marathoner, triathlete, "extreme sports" competitor, or some other hobby or activity requiring an unusually high level of commitment. Employers tend to look at such activities as competitors for your time and distractions from your work. They will admire your mental and physical stamina, but will not hire you unless they are into the same activities. Curiously, Neil has also found it unwise to put "pursuing my master's degree while working full time" on a resume. Most employers tend to focus more on time-off issues than academic self improvement. However, Neil has not found this to be the case with bachelor's degrees.

> *Resumes, like a fine suit, should be carefully tailored to the person who will be interviewing you and to the company and position you are interviewing for.*

Incidentally, the candidate with the doctorate in business had sent his resume to dozens of manufacturing companies and hadn't had a single interview, and could not understand why. "These companies should be jumping all over themselves to interview me! How many people are out there with my qualifications?" For Neil, the answer was obvious: "None," including the rough-and-tumble plant managers he was sending his resume to. How many of these people want to interview someone with a Ph.D., an "egghead," as one plant manager had termed Ph.D.s?

As soon as he took "Ph.D." off his resume, he started getting responses. The MBA he also had was something of value to these plant managers. Neil advised him to mention the fact that he had a Ph.D. only at a time when he was certain it would add value to his candidacy, such as if the company needed someone to do a research project which nobody presently on staff was qualified to take on but by hiring him, the company would save the expense of a consultant.

11. Everyone is interviewing you.

From the moment you meet someone even remotely associated with your interview, you are being evaluated. The "I'm just the driver" person who greets you at the airport, the receptionist, the person at the company cafeteria cash register, the hotel desk clerk who knows which company you are the guest of, even the person who was in the company restroom when you were in there and not a word was spoken. All are potential evaluators who can assist or sink your candidacy. (Neil has a recruiter friend who lost a placement because a candidate did not wash his hands after using the restroom.) Be very polite, friendly, and nice to everyone, from the moment you leave your home to the time you return to it after the interview. When you leave the interview and the company gathers all the people together who met you, you do not want someone saying that you treated him or her rudely.

12. If you want the job, ask for it.

It always amazes us how so few interview candidates have heard this statement before: "If you want the job, tell them plainly that you want it." In all of Neil's time in the placement business, job candidates have rarely asked for the job, which is one of the most powerful tools they can use. Most believe they asked for the job with statements they made during the interview such as "I am extremely interested" and "I know I could do this job well" and similar declarations. However, they have not actually asked for the job. They have done what all the other candidates are doing: saying every combination of words except "I want this position." The reasons for this vary, but the most common reason is fear, and it is not a fear of rejection, which one would think was the case. We have found that most candidates are afraid of being offered the job. Seems strange, but it really isn't. People are naturally afraid of change and of commitment. To tell an interviewer plainly that you want the position and then to receive it on the spot implies that you are now obligated to go to work for that employer because the employer did what was asked of him. That is not the case.

Some candidates don't ask for the position they want because they are afraid of appearing too eager and thus losing leverage when it comes time to negotiate an offer. They may think that once a company knows you want to work for it, the company will make an offer that is less than it could have been had the candidate played "hard to get." As mentioned earlier, that is one of the biggest job interviewing myths, and it has caused the loss of many great opportunities. What manager wants to have someone come aboard and then become angry and possibly quit the company three months into the job when he discovers he was "low-balled" in offer negotiations? Such information always leaks out eventually. We have found that most hiring managers make fair, reasonable, and generous offers because they want the new person to arrive in the new position excited and enthusiastic.

> *Most hiring managers make fair, reasonable, and generous offers because they want the new person to arrive in the new position excited and enthusiastic.*

Whatever the reason for not asking directly for the position you want, candidates who do ask have the edge because they're doing something positive that the other candidates are not doing. It's extremely powerful and positive when a candidate shakes hands to say good-bye to the interviewer, looks him straight in the eyes, and states in a confident, matter-of-fact voice:

> *"From what we have discussed today, and from what you have shown me about this company and position, I feel confident that this is the right place for*

> *me. I know I could do a great job for you, and I would be honored to join your*
> *team. What do we need to do to put this together?"*

Under most circumstances, it is rare that an employer will respond by offering the position on the spot. However, it does happen occasionally. If that happens, accept the offer on the spot if it's a good offer, or ask for the evening to "sleep on it." At a minimum, when the employer sits down to evaluate his finalist candidates, among close competition, the one who showed the most desire for the position will have the edge, and that person is the one who asked for the job.

One more thing: You should only ask for the position with the interviewer who would be the direct reporting supervisor for the position. This is the person who makes the final decision on hires, not the Human Resources manager or some other individual.

Final Review and Preparation

We've only covered a fraction of what could be written about interviewing. We've revealed the minimum information necessary to do well on an interview. In fact, if you do only what is written here, you will do well on your interview. For more in-depth information on interviewing, including coverage of different types of interviews such as behavior-based and situational interviews and job interviewing for ex-offenders and others with not-so-hot backgrounds, see Ron's five comprehensive job interview books:

- *The Ex-Offender's Job Interview Guide*
- *I Can't Believe They Asked Me That!*
- *Job Interview Tips for People With Not-So-Hot Backgrounds*
- *Win the Interview, Win the Job*
- *You Should Hire Me!*

Here is a final review of the interview process:

1. **Before the interview**

   Research the company and interviewers in depth. Get on the Internet and bring up the company's website and read every page on that site. Familiarize yourself with all the products, services, and philosophy of the company. Most companies have their mission statement on their websites – learn it. Also, check out the company using different search engines, and proceed through each with the company's name and also the name(s) of the person(s) who will be interviewing you. You will be amazed how most people of any note have at least something on the Internet about them, probably including yourself! If the interviewer has published a magazine article, written a book, or given a speech, read everything you can find. (Interviewers are always impressed when a candidate has read something they have written or said.)

   Know the basic financial information of the company, whether it's a public or private company, its sales volume, and recent stock price history. Be able to answer the "What do you know about us?" question with at least five significant facts about the company.

Prepare a two-minute "career summary" answer to the "Tell me about yourself" question. Remember, that is the most frequently asked icebreaker question, but it can kill your candidacy right at the start because you need to understand what the interviewer is looking for before giving details. Unless otherwise directed by the interviewer, your answer should be a simple chronological history of your career positions. Give no personal information, do not rush or ramble, and then close with:

"This brings us to today. What are some of the duties and responsibilities of the position?"

or say

"What are some of the problems and needs of the company that you want someone to solve for you?"

Remember: You **must** know what the interviewer's needs are before you give detailed answers!

Prepare a list of your three most significant professional achievements. Have a mini-story for each...a two-minute account using the S.O.A.R. approach (**S**ituation, **O**bjective, **A**ction my team took under my leadership, and **R**esults achieved).

Put together a list of your three greatest strengths, and one weakness. Prepare specific examples for each. For the weakness, you should follow it by saying "But this is what I have done to work on it..." It is better to have a weakness than to say you can't think of any!

Practice this script for the "How much money do you want?" question:

"Although money is important, it is not the most important thing to me because I also consider the position, the company, and the overall opportunity, all of which look great here. Also, I am unfamiliar with how XYZ Company would compensate someone with my background and experience. I've got [X] years doing the kinds of things you need done. What would you offer someone with my background and experience?"

Never reject anything! If you think the offer is weak, tell him or her you would have to think it over. Then do your research on salary comparables to see what you may need to do to strengthen that offer with a counter-offer. And **never** bring up or ask questions about compensation, benefits, vacation, work hours, or other such "creature comfort" items first; wait until after the company brings them up or after you have received an offer.

Have a "latest book read" and "latest movie seen" prepared. Make certain they are biographical-type stories of achievement and greatness, or are on a business theme, not a love story, science fiction, or other frivolous topic unless you are interviewing with a company that is known to value such thinking. If necessary, see a good movie and read a compelling book if you have to in order to tell the truth successfully on that question.

Tailor your resume to the interviewer, company, and position. Bring a few original paper copies of your resume to the interview.

If you are a man interviewing for a professional position, wear a conservative single-breasted suit. Unless you are a senior executive, do not wear tie tacks, a handkerchief, cuff links, or "personalized" dress shirts. Shave off facial hair. If you are transitioning military, do not wear any uniform items whatsoever, nor wear a miniaturization of the ribbon of your highest medal. (You should put your most distinguished medal award on your resume, not your lapel.) Have shined shoes, and wear socks that match your trousers.

If you are a woman, wear business attire. Do not wear a dress unless you're interviewing for a clerical or office support position.

If you are interviewing for a nonprofessional position, you should wear what is considered appropriate attire for someone in that position and with that particular company. Always wear neat, clean, and conservative clothes. Your attire should never be a distraction during the interview nor an issue when it comes time to make another interview or hiring decision.

Finally, neither men nor women should wear conspicuous jewelry, body piercings, or allow tattoos to be visible. The rule is this: An interview is not the place to wear anything that makes a statement about your individuality unless the person hiring is publicly known to value such people.

Practice the most important script of all: the Interview Closing Sequence. Practice it until it is as natural as breathing. No matter how messed up an interview gets, if you are given a second appointment before you leave the building, you have been successful!

2. During the interview

When you arrive at the company, give your name to the reception area attendant and let him or her know who you are scheduled to meet. You may be given an application to fill out. Fill out every block completely, and do not put "see resume" anywhere on it. For "Salary desired" write "Open" or "Negotiable." For "Have you even been convicted of a felony?" leave blank or write "Will discuss at the interview."

When you meet the interviewer, give a good, firm handshake, state your name, and smile. Build rapport, break the ice, but don't give out much information on anything until you understand the nature of the position you are interviewing for. Ask the interviewer for this critical information! Give strong examples of your achievements and accomplishments as they relate to the company's needs. Illustrate what you bring to the company with specifics – not generalities such as "hard-working team player." (Who isn't a "hard-working team player"??)

Be original, outgoing, friendly, and conversational. Avoid being a quiet introvert just sitting there passively answering questions. Show the interviewer that you are an enthusiastic problem-solver who can not only do the job that is open, but by hiring you, the company will be getting someone who can do more than fill a specific opening on an organization chart. If the position is being created or is unclear, ask questions regarding problems and issues facing the company or department, and offer solutions.

Do not hand over your resume unless it is requested. After all, you don't want the interviewer reading your resume while you're talking, or, worse, find yourself in an awkward silence while he is reading. If he requests the resume, give it to him and allow about three minutes for him or her to read it before inquiring about the needs of the company. That's because the interviewer is forming an opinion of you while reading your resume, and people tend to think a resume lists all your experience, and if their specific "buzz word" isn't on it, then you lack that experience. You **must** get the interviewer to discuss the needs and problems to be solved and to not judge your ability by your resume alone.

Turn off your cell phone; do not simply put it on "silent" mode! Carry a small notepad, PDA, or electronic day planner. (Do not bring a briefcase!)

Do not take notes except when the interviewer says something you must remember, such as a name, date, or something similar. Many books say that candidates in interviews should take notes. We disagree. What good are those notes if you don't get a second interview? Employers have told Neil they feel distracted by note-taking. Also, note-taking slows down the flow of the conversation, which is awkward in itself.

As we have said repeatedly, do not leave until you and the interviewer have agreed to a specific date and time for the next meeting! Use the Interview Closing Sequence scheduling technique. It is the most important part of interviewing successfully!

If you want the job, say so to the interviewer who would be your supervisor. Tell him or her in a straightforward, businesslike, decisive manner. That is quite different from "groveling." Demonstrate to the interviewer that you are a confident, clear-thinking, "cut to the bottom line" individual who can handle both good and bad news.

3. After the interview

Write and email a thank-you note to everyone who came in contact with you, and write the notes within an hour after leaving the interview! Write each note with a touch of originality, and include a personal recollection for each reader. (Pay attention to the small talk at the beginning of each interview – that is where you will get most of your personal information for the notes!) Avoid such overused phrases as "thank you for taking time out from your busy day…" Try to email as soon as possible your thank-you notes. If you don't have a computer, go immediately to a library or an Internet café and use their computers. Speed is imperative in this matter. You want the people who met you to receive your thank-you notes

before they get together to discuss you, which could be anytime after your interview. This way, when the interviewers get together to discuss you, the subject of everyone receiving a note from you will certainly come up. They will then compare the notes with the expectation that all the notes will be exactly the same, which is the usual case for almost all candidates, and therefore not impressive. When they see that each of your notes was uniquely tailored to each individual, they will be favorably impressed! If one of the interviewers was about to give a less-than-enthusiastic report on you, seeing all the others glowing about you will put subtle pressure on this person to change his report so as to not appear to be out of step with the key leaders in the company. Thank-you notes can make the hire! Lack of them will "break" the hire!

If you have been given something to fill out or complete, such as an application, test, or other document, or there is something the company has asked you to do, do it immediately. When a company gives you something to do, it is measuring how long it takes you to respond. An application or any paperwork given to you after the interview should be filled out in the lobby and left with the receptionist before you return to your car. If that is not possible because of travel arrangements, then you should fill it out the same day and then return it to the company via overnight mail (FedEx, UPS, or Express Mail) so it arrives the next day.

Never allow more than 24 hours to pass between your interview and the return of an application, document, resume, test, or whatever it is the company asked you to complete. Other candidates will take longer than 24 hours; this is another way for you to distinguish yourself from the pack.

Appendix B

Answering and Asking Key Questions

"Express your interest, drive, initiative, and enthusiasm in the questions you both answer and ask."

MUCH OF ONE'S SUCCESS in getting a job offer is the ability to both answer and ask key questions. In this section we identify some of the questions most frequently asked by interviewers. We also include a list of thoughtful questions you should ask during the interview.

Most Frequently Asked Questions

The following questions are frequently asked by interviewers. Indeed, you should be able to predict 95 percent of the questions that are likely to be asked in most interviews. Use this appendix as a handy checklist to prepare for your next interview.

As you plan responses to each question, remember to formulate a **strategy**. You should not try to formulate the exact words you would use and then memorize them. To do this would be a big mistake. At best your answer would likely sound canned and you would greatly diminish your credibility. At worst, you might forget your memorized response in the middle of your answer!

So consider your answers in terms of basic strategies. What do you hope to convey as you respond to each question? Your goal is to convince the interviewer that you should be offered the job. As you get ready to respond, think in terms of the **needs** of the employer. How do your goals fit with her business needs? Keep this basic tenet in mind as you formulate your strategies in response to questions you are asked. Try to make time prior to the interview to actually talk through your answers to questions. You may practice answering interview questions (which you have made into a list) posed by a friend or family member or you can read each question and then respond. Practice talking your answers into a tape recorder. Play back the tape and evaluate how you sound:

- Do you exude confidence?
- Do you sound dynamic?

- Do you talk in a conversational style? (rather than your response sounding mechanical)
- Do you speak without excessive fillers such as *"ah," "and uh," "like,"* and *"you know"*?
- Do you seem believable?
- Do you appear likable?

Try to give your best response to each of the following questions using a tape recorder. Then listen to your recorded responses and critique them.

Each time you talk through an answer, your words will be somewhat different since you have purposely not tried to memorize your response. You have thought through the strategy of your response, the gist of the message you want to convey, but you have not attempted to commit a response to memory.

Personality and Motivation

1. Why should we hire you?

2. Are you a self-starter?

3. What is your greatest strength?

4. What is your greatest weakness?

5. What would you most like to improve about yourself?

6. What are some of the reasons for your success?

7. Describe your typical workday.

8. Do you anticipate problems or do you react to them?

9. How do you deal with stressful situations?

10. Do you ever lose your temper?

11. How well do you work under deadlines?

12. What contributions did you make to your last (or present) company?

13. What will you bring to this position that others won't?

14. How well do you get along with your superiors?

15. How well do you get along with your co-workers?

16. How do you manage your subordinates?

17. How do you feel about working with superiors who may have less education than you?

18. Do you prefer working alone or with others?

19. How do others view your work?

20. How do you deal with criticism?

21. Do you consider yourself to be someone who takes greater initiative than others?

22. Do you consider yourself a risk-taker?

23. Are you a good time manager?

24. How important is job security?

25. How do you define success?

26. How do you spend your leisure time?

27. What would be the perfect job for you?

28. What really motivates you to perform on the job?

29. How old are you?

30. What does your spouse think about your career?

31. Are you living with anyone?

32. Do you have many debts?

33. Do you own or rent your home?

34. What social or political organizations do you belong to?

Education and Training

35. Why didn't you go to college?

36. Why didn't you finish college?

37. Why did you select _____ college?

38. Why did you major in _____?

39. What was your minor in school?

40. How did your major relate to the work you have done since graduation?

41. Why weren't your grades better in school?

42. What subjects did you enjoy most?

43. What subjects did you enjoy least?

44. If you could go back and do it over again, what would you change about your college education?

45. What extracurricular activities did you participate in during college?

46. Tell me about your role in (<u>one of your extracurricular activities</u>).

47. What leadership positions did you hold in college?

48. How did your degree prepare you for the job at _____?

49. Did you work part time or full time while you were in college?

50. Are you planning to take additional courses or start graduate school over the next year or two?

51. If you had a choice of several short training sessions to attend, which two or three would you select?

52. What materials do you read regularly to keep up with what is going on in your field?

53. What is the most recent skill you have learned?

54. What are your educational goals over the next few years?

Experience and Skills

55. Why do you want to leave your present job or previous jobs?

56. Why have you changed jobs so frequently?

57. Why would you be more likely to stay here?

58. What are your qualifications for this job?

59. What experience prepares you for this job?

60. What did you like most about your present/most recent job?

61. What did you like least about that job?

62. What did you like most about your boss?

63. What did you like least about that boss?

64. Tell me about an ongoing responsibility in your current/most recent job that you enjoyed.

65. How does your present job (or most recent) relate to the overall goals of your department/the company?

66. What has your present/most recent supervisor(s) criticized about your work?

67. What duties in your present/most recent job do you find it difficult to do?

68. Why do you want to leave your present job? Are you being forced out?

69. Why should we hire someone like you – with your experience and motivation?

70. What type of person would you hire for this position?

71. Have you ever been fired or asked to resign?

72. What was the most important contribution you made on your last job?

73. What do you wish you had accomplished in your present/most recent job but were unable to?

74. What is the most important thing you've learned from the jobs you've held?

Career Goals

75. Tell me about yourself.

76. Tell me about your career goals.

77. What would you like to accomplish during the next five years (or ten years).

78. How do your career goals today differ from your career goals five years ago?

79. Where do you see yourself five years from now?

80. Describe a major goal you set for yourself recently?

81. What are you doing to achieve that goal?

82. Have you ever thought of switching careers?

83. How does this job compare to what would be the perfect job for you?

84. What would you change about our company to make this your ideal work-place?

85. How long have you been looking for another job?

Why You Want This Job

86. What do you know about our company?

87. What trends do you see in our industry?

88. Why do you want to work for us?

89. How much business would you bring to our firm?

90. What similarities do you see between this and your current/most recent position?

91. What makes this position different from your current/most recent position?

92. Why are you willing to take a job you are over-qualified for?

93. Why are you willing to take a pay cut from your previous (present position)?

94. What would you change about this position?

95. How long would you expect to stay with our company?

96. How do you feel about working overtime or on weekends?

97. Are you willing to relocate?

98. How much are you willing to travel?

99. What are your salary expectations?

100. How soon could you begin work?

101. Do you have any questions?

Unexpected Questions

You may not be asked any questions beyond the ones outlined above. If the questions you are asked do go beyond these, they will most likely fall into one of two categories:

- Specific questions that relate to special knowledge or skills required for the job for which you are being considered.

- Questions that are raised by unusual items or unexplained gaps or omissions on your resume or application.

Look over your resume. Is there anything that stands out? If you spent the last three years in prison but indicate under "Experience" that you worked for the State of Ohio, which you honestly did, the interviewer may want to probe the type of state job you held. If you have a two- to five-year unexplained gap in your work history, this gap is bound to raise the question of what you were doing during this time. You need to be ready with honest, yet positive answers, that will further promote your candidacy rather than knock you out of the running.

If you have thoughtfully considered your responses and practiced responding with the gist of the message you want to convey, these questions should not throw you. However, if you haven't given such questions much thought, your responses are likely to show it.

Few questions should ever be answered with a mere *"yes"* or *"no."* Remember to provide **examples** as often as possible to support the points you make. If asked by the interviewer whether you are a self-starter, you could simply respond *"yes."* However you score few points for this response. It really says nothing except that either you think you are a self-starter, or you think this is the response the interviewer wants to hear. But if you follow your *"yes"* response with an example or two of what you did that demonstrates you were a self-starter in your last job, you start to sell yourself. You want to impress the interviewer and you want to stand out from the rest of the applicants being interviewed.

Remember to **use examples** and use them frequently. Examples support assertions about your abilities and thus help sell you to the interviewer. Examples make what you say about your skills and achievements more clear, more interesting, more credible, and more likely to be remembered. They help tell your **story**.

Behavior- and Situation-Based Questions

Employers are increasingly incorporating behavior-based and situation-based questions in job interviews. "Behavior-based" means that the interviewer asks you to describe how you responded when you faced an actual situation. "Hypothetical situational-based" questions don't ask for an actual situation, but ask you to imagine a situation and describe how you would act if that occurred. These types of interview questions are an attempt to get applicants to do what they should be doing anyway: expanding their answers with examples that support the assertions they are making.

Be prepared to respond to these types of open-ended behavior-based and situation-based questions:

1. What would you do if . . .
2. In what situations have you become so involved in the work you were doing that the day flew by?
3. If you were to encounter that same situation now, how would you deal with that person?
4. If you had a choice of working in our department A or department B, which would you choose?
5. Why would you make that choice?
6. Tell me about a recent time when you took responsibility for a task that was outside of our job description.
7. Tell me about a time when you took action without your supervisor's prior approval.

Questions You Should Ask

One of the most important questions you can answer is that last one on our list of 101 questions – *"Do you have any questions?"* The answer should be *"Yes, I have a few questions."* No matter how thorough the interview, no matter how much give-and-take, you should have at least two or three questions to ask near the end of the interview. Not asking any questions may hurt your chances of getting the job offer. During the interview other questions will probably come to mind which you had not anticipated.

When asked whether you have questions, you may indicate that many have been answered thus far, but you have a few additional questions. You should have jotted some questions down as you prepared for your interview. Feel free to refer to that list if you need to at this point. The fact that you have given thought to this aspect of the interview and have come prepared will be viewed as a positive by the interviewer. You may have questions, for example, about the relationship of this job to other significant functional areas in the company, staff

> *You should have at least two or three questions to ask near the end of the interview.*

development, training programs, career advancement opportunities, the extent to which promotions are from within the organization, how employee performance is evaluated, or the expected growth of the company. You may want to ask questions that probe areas that were touched on earlier during the interview. For example, if the interviewer has mentioned that the company has an excellent training program, you may have specific questions: What kinds of training would you be offered? How frequently? How long do most training programs last?

Most employers are not interested in hiring closed-minded individuals who don't listen and follow directives. They look for interest, drive, initiative, and enthusiasm – personal qualities that can be expressed through the questions you ask during the interview.

Prospective employers expect you will have to learn about their operations. If you listen very carefully to what the interviewer says, you should pick up clues as to specific needs of the employer. You want to identify what problems the company faces as well as learn about possible solutions appropriate to the company. Be careful in offering solutions to problems you do not understand and a company you are unfamiliar with. Your proposed solutions may appear naive or, even worse, offend certain well-established employees who are not particularly interested in hiring an outsider. Keep an open mind by asking questions about how the interviewer and others in the organization view the problem as well as the solution. Learn as much as possible about the internal operation of the organization, especially the key players with whom you will work and who will influence your work life. Ask some of these questions to gain knowledge about the interpersonal dynamics of the position:

- Whom will I be working with?
- Can you tell me something about them and their work?
- How long have they been with the company?
- Of all the people I'll be working with, which ones do you consider to be most reliable?
- Whom would you recommend I turn to for assistance?
- What do you see as the major problems related to my position?
- Will I be replacing someone or is this a new position?

- Can you tell me about the person who last held this position?
- How long did he stay?
- Why did he leave?
- Would it be okay if I talked to him about this position?
- What might he tell me, or not tell me?
- What issues did he face and how did he deal with them?
- Were you generally pleased with his work?
- Are there certain potholes here that I should be aware of?
- What do you see as your biggest challenges ahead?
- How does my position relate to those challenges?
- Can you tell me a little more about how you plan to solve these problems?
- What has been done so far?
- What other ideas have been considered?

This line of questioning impresses upon the interviewer that you are an inquisitive person who listens and is open to others' ideas. You are interested in learning from others before drawing conclusions and making decisions. In other words, you have a non-threatening personality, one that might fit well with other personalities in the organization.

If you are still interested in this job, be sure to close the interview by summarizing the strong points you would bring to the position and indicate your continued interest in the job and the company. Ask what the next step will be and when they expect to make a decision.

Ask Yourself These Questions

1. **Which job interview questions do I feel most uncomfortable answering?**

_____

_____

_____

_____

_____

2. **Why would someone want to hire me?**

_____

_____

_____

_____

_____

3. **How can I best answer this initial question: "Tell me about yourself."**

_____

_____

_____

_____

4. **What are my three greatest strengths that I would bring to the workplace?**

_____

_____

_____

_____

5. **Which red-flag questions might I be asked based upon reviewing my re-sume and/or application?**_____

_____

_____

_____

_____

6. **What questions should I ask the interviewer?**_____

_____

_____

_____

_____

Appendix C

Leaving With Professionalism

"When it's time to go, make a positive exit that will always leave the door open."

THIS APPENDIX IS DESIGNED for individuals who are currently employed and need to make a graceful exit from their employer. If you are not employed at present, you can skip this section altogether.

You have made the decision to resign from your present employer. The reasons for this decision have been well thought out, even though you realize how hard it will be to leave your friends and the people with whom you have shared much. However, you evaluated all the pros and cons, and you made the decision because you know deep inside that you will not be satisfied working in your present organization for the "long haul." You knew that sooner or later you would be leaving, and so you've decided to resolve the issue. It's time to leave and not allow an opportunity to slip away due to fear of change or inaction.

Feelings

Moving to a new job or career is always stressful, even when someone dislikes his or her present employer! If a new job involves relocation, then the anxiety factor is increased even more. Those butterflies in the stomach, those sleepless nights wondering whether a mistake is being made, those headaches from thinking about all the details of making the career move, and that general feeling of uncertainty – all can be uncomfortable and seem difficult to manage at times. However, people who accomplish much in life do not allow such emotions to keep them from moving forward. In fact, many people who were leaving the military told Neil that their fear of a new career was more intense than when they were deployed in combat! It should be encouraging to know that although these emotions are uncomfortable, they are also completely normal. Additionally, they are also almost always temporary and will subside almost immediately after a very short time in your new job (usually within a few days in the new company). In all Neil's years of placing people in hundreds of new positions, only an extremely small number (five, to be precise) believed they had made a mistake after they reported to their new job. All the rest were extremely glad they had made the change to a new company and position. Even the five who felt they had made a mistake adjusted quickly to their new surroundings and soon developed a rhythm and routine which eliminated those uncomfortable feelings. Due to the emotionally demanding nature of change, never give more than two weeks notice to an employer you are leaving. Regardless of how high up in an organization one is or how much his or her supervisor pleads or implies it is "the ethical thing to do" to give a longer notice, one should **never** give more than two weeks notice when leaving a company. Two weeks notice is the universally accepted, and expected, time standard for a resignation in American business. Regarding notice periods longer than two weeks, we have observed some people who believed (erroneously) that the more time they took to "relax" before starting employment with their new company, the less stress would be involved with the change. In theory, that seems to make sense. In reality, however, the longer time they took to start the new job, the more preoccupied they felt because they were thinking about their new job the entire time they thought they'd be relaxing! The solution is always to get established in the new company as quickly as possible, and put the change behind you. Get familiar with the organization, become confident with your new responsibilities, and soon you will feel that great inner peace at knowing deep down that you made a great move! Once your transition anxiety subsides, as it will, you will experience a tremendous feeling of accomplishment when you realize that you successfully "made the break" to a great opportunity. To get to that accomplishment, however, will require that you take certain actions and steps involved with your resignation and actual departure from your present company, and to do so in a manner that is professional, thoughtful, and leaves all with whom you have worked admiring you.

The Steps to Resigning

Your departure from your present company will involve at least four components:

1. The resignation letter
2. The resignation meeting with your supervisors
3. Your announcement to your co-workers that you are leaving
4. Your final day at the company when you actually walk out the door.

The Resignation Letter

Your **resignation letter** should be a short, one-page formal memo to your supervisor, and it should be the first notification to anyone (except your family) that you are resigning. It should be placed on his or her desk in an envelope marked "confidential," or sent as an email with the letter as an attachment if your manager is at a distant location. Do not copy anyone on the letter or email. If it is an email, make certain to include receipt verification. The letter should:

1. Begin with a statement that you have accepted a new position.

2. Followed by a statement designating your last day with the company, a date no more than two weeks from the date of the letter.

3. Closing with a brief positive statement about the company and your supervisor, that you will help find your replacement, that your decision was a difficult one to make, and that you would appreciate the company respecting your decision by not attempting to persuade you to stay.

Here is a sample resignation letter:

> *To: Josephine Smith, General Manager, ABC Corporation*
>
> *From: Bill Jones, Plant Manager*
>
> *Subject: Resignation*
>
> *Date: April 19th, 2016*
>
> *Dear Josephine:*
>
> *After much thought and careful consideration, I have accepted a sales position with XYZ Corporation with a start date of Monday, May 5th, 2016. My last day of employment with ABC Company shall be Friday, May 2nd, 2016.*
>
> *I want you to know that my decision has nothing to do with ABC Company or with you as my supervisor. You have been a great leader and mentor to me, and I hope that my future supervisors will be as professionally concerned with my development as you have been. I simply believe that this new opportunity with XYZ Company is better for my career growth and that it is the right move for me.*
>
> *Departing from ABC Company is difficult for me, and so I ask that the Company respect my decision and not make it more difficult than it already is. Attempting to persuade me to remain here would make it harder for me, so I ask only for your good wishes, which is what I extend to you and the team. I will miss you all.*
>
> *Finally, I will be happy to assist in any way I can at finding my replacement during my two-week transition period and also after I leave, on a non-interference basis with my new employer.*
>
> *Thank you for your understanding of this sensitive matter.*
>
> *Sincerely,*
>
> *Bill Jones*

The Resignation Meeting

The meeting with your manager, which is often referred to as the "exit interview," could come at any time after submission of your resignation letter – perhaps immediately, perhaps a few days later. Whenever it is, it is not the time to show uncertainty with your decision, even if you feel uncertain.

This is the point in time where emotions can lead to poor judgment, so be very careful here. If you are a valued team member, your manager is going to be disappointed with your resignation, and he/she may attempt to persuade you to stay. This can be very flattering and appear well meaning at the time, but it is really not for the employee's benefit as it might appear, but rather for the manager's benefit. Why? Because what this manager is really trying to do is called "damage control." He or she is attempting to change your mind about leaving before others learn of the decision. Managers do not like to lose good people. If a pattern develops where too many people leave a particular executive's department, it will be noticed by top management, and that manager may soon be joining the departing employees.

A true leader will never attempt to cause a subordinate to doubt a decision as important and emotionally draining as changing employers. That is similar to questioning someone's judgment in selection of a spouse, purchase of a new home, or some other major decision. Nor will a person with sound business ethics ever attempt to persuade someone to not show up at his or her new company. Managers know better than anyone how tough it is to recruit good people and make a hiring selection, and also how damaging it can be when someone does not report for work, often setting an entire organization back. To deliberately put another manager at another organization is not only unethical, but also unscrupulous.

Good leaders are also supportive of the decisions of their subordinates. They will express regret at a resignation, ask why the person is leaving, but once they hear that the decision is final, they will no longer press the issue. They will say something like this:

> *"You are always welcome here. I wish you the best always, continued success in your new job, and I would be glad to support you with references or anything else I can provide. Good luck and let me know how things are going for you once you get your feet on the ground in your new assignment. Stay in touch."*

If you are unfortunate and have a self-serving manager, or one you thought was good but is now showing signs of questionable ethics, you need to use extreme caution. You are in a vulnerable state of mind because of the stress of a venture into the unknown, and this person knows it. No matter how personally or professionally close you are with this type of person, once you submit a resignation, this person will manipulate the situation to his/her benefit. The resignation meeting is usually the best time for an attempt to persuade you to withdraw your resignation or, at a minimum, get you to question the wisdom of your decision and/or consider extending or delaying your notice period. You are going to hear such statements as:

> "Let me at least have a few weeks to see what I can do to fix things. Surely, if your new company (or 'that recruiter') has your best interests at heart, he or she will not object to allowing you more time to make sure you are making the right decision." **(The "best interest" to buy time tactic.)**

> "Look, there are some things I could not tell you regarding your future here. You are being flagged by top management to take over this department (or that project). But if you don't stick around, you won't see how things play out." **(The "confidential big plans" tactic.)**

> "You say you want to leave because of (reason). Don't you think it's only fair to me, someone who has developed you and mentored you over the years, to allow me an opportunity to correct that situation before you decide to leave us?" **(The "guilt" tactic.)**

"I am to blame for all this. I should have been more in touch with your needs, and probably should be more in touch with the others as well. In fact, I have probably been a complete tyrant and totally oblivious to it. Do this for me: before making your final decision, give me some time to prove to you and the others that I can change. Sometimes it takes losing someone of great value to realize just how much people matter." (**The "Ebenezer Scrooge" tactic.**)

The limits to the approaches that can be made are only as limited as a manager's creativity, but the bottom line is this: Never resign from a company unless you are really going to leave, no matter what the company says, does, or promises to convince you to stay.

Here are only five of the many risks associated with remaining at a company after resignation: **First**, your resignation will be an unpleasant surprise for your manager, and will come at the worst time possible. As with any adverse surprise for someone, he or she will react by saying or doing whatever is necessary to temporarily relieve the problem. Like a boat with a hole and water rushing in, whatever it takes to stop the flood is what will be attempted. However, once the shock wears off, your manager will begin to regret what was promised to you. Over time, resentment towards you will grow within your manager. You will now have a higher probability of being fired for a superficial reason. Also, once your peers and co-workers learn what happened, they will also resent you because they will think you were rewarded for your disloyalty.

Second, you will never again be trusted at your company. In your manager's mind, and in the eyes of your co-workers, you were disloyal. To them, you were lying to everyone when you called in sick to go on interviews. They will also always wonder what negative things you said about them and the company when you were asked in your interviews why you were planning to leave. To your company, why should you ever again be considered an "up and comer" when you have proved that you are not happy with the company? Your manager and peers will always wonder what you really think, say, and feel about them. In the future, whenever you want time off, or you really are ill, your manager and co-workers will wonder if you are being truthful. It is never the same, and as time goes by, you will feel increasingly angry with yourself that you did not leave the company when you had the chance.

Third, almost all offers intended to persuade someone to not leave are stall tactics designed to buy the time necessary to find a permanent solution to a new problem, i.e., time to secretly find your replacement. When a key person submits a resignation, no company can afford to risk having a hole where that person was, or even uncertainty as to the work getting done for which that person was responsible.

Fourth, in tough times, who do you think will be the first to be laid off? If someone who has never resigned is laid off before someone who had resigned and was reinstated, the entire company will become disgruntled.

Finally, we have spoken with business leaders who had made the mistake of convincing someone who had resigned to remain. Most told us, "I could not allow this person to go. He or she was simply too important to the company (or "program" or "project") to allow leaving." ALL these business leaders said they soon regretted persuading the person to remain, and looked for reasons to terminate the person in question, especially when co-workers found out what happened. The most prevalent reason was stated succinctly: "From that point on, I felt as though he thought he was the boss, not me. Each time I would ask him to perform a difficult task; he would look as me as if he had a choice. I wanted him out!" There are many other reasons never to consider remaining with a company after resigning. However, if you consider staying, be sure to write up a new employment contract that includes at least six months of severance pay in the event of your termination, and have your boss sign it. If your manager won't do this, what does that tell you? Can you really afford to work in a place where you will never know when the "axe will fall"? Some companies ask people to leave the moment they resign. That is not necessarily a bad thing. In fact, it is probably better because it will get you out of a now awkward existence where you are neither "in" nor "out." If you are asked to leave immediately, call your new company and move up your start date and put the transition period behind you.

Dealing With Your Peers and Subordinates

You should get the word of your resignation out to your peers and subordinates immediately after you have made certain your boss has received your resignation. That's because they have a stake in what you do, and you do not want them to worry about their own futures, so inform them early on. However, never inform anyone that you are leaving until after you have given your manager your resignation. To do so would be a major disservice to them. Never speak negatively about anyone, no matter how much you believe people will agree with you. Your statements will get back to those people involved, and that will ruin your references. It could also get you in legal trouble. The best approach is a short answer. When people ask why you are leaving, answer by saying you are leaving "for a great opportunity." Add nothing more. The rule of thumb is this: To leave professionally, the less you say, the better off you are. It also makes you appear "classy." That is why famous and important people give very little information when they leave organizations.

During your two-week notice period, do not be surprised if you feel like an outsider, awkward, and possibly even avoided at your company. Do not take it personally. In fact, make an effort to take your close friends aside privately or call them after hours and let them know that you want to keep your distance from them for their sake, as you do not want their supervisors to think that they, too, are planning to leave. Your friends will appreciate that.

Perhaps the company will throw a farewell party or lunch for you. Be gracious and give a two-minute "thank you, everyone" speech at the event. If you desire to give a longer speech, make it no longer than five minutes, use some humor, but do not "roast" anyone. Because this is a departure speech, you do not want people to think such "roast" comments are your "true" negative feelings about people at that company. Keep things lighthearted.

For most people, the two-week notice period is a time of reflection, sadness (even if they hated their job!), and possibly high anxiety. It can be a very tough time emotionally, even for the strongest person. The longer one has been with a company, the more significant the emotions can be during this period. You may even experience moments when you feel as though you are making a big mistake. Do not give in to those feelings if they occur. Breathe deeply...take a walk around the building...they will pass. **Never** prolong the transition period for longer than is absolutely necessary, and that's why you should never give more than two weeks notice. On your last day at the company, go to each person at the company, including those with whom you may have had disagreements or may not have liked personally. Wish each and every one of them your sincere best wishes for the future. Leave with everyone admiring you. Leave professionally!!

Index

Re-Entry Success Resources

THE FOLLOWING RE-ENTRY RESOURCES are available from Impact Publications. Full descriptions of each as well as downloadable catalogs and video clips can be found at www.impactpublications.com. Complete the following form or list the titles, include shipping (see formula at the end), enclose payment, and send your order to:

IMPACT PUBLICATIONS
9104 Manassas Drive, Suite N
Manassas Park, VA 20111-5211
1-800-361-1055 (orders only)
Tel. 703-361-7300 or Fax 703-335-9486
Email: query@impactpublications.com
Quick & easy online ordering: www.impactpublications.com

Orders from individuals must be prepaid by check, money order, or major credit card. We accept telephone, fax, and email orders. Since prices may change, please verify online www.impactpublications.com before ordering.

Qty.	TITLES	Price	TOTAL
Featured Title			
_____	The Ex-Offender's 30/30 Job Solution	$11.95	_____
Re-Entry Pocket Guides (quantity discounts featured on inside cover page)			
_____	The Anger Management Pocket Guide	$2.95	_____
_____	Re-Entry Employment & Life Skills Pocket Guide	2.95	_____
_____	Re-Entry Personal Finance Pocket Guide	2.95	_____
_____	Re-Entry Start-Up Pocket Guide (see page 124)	2.95	_____
_____	Re-Imagining Life on the Outside Pocket Guide	2.95	_____
Re-Entry and Survival for Ex-Offenders			
_____	9 to 5 Beats Ten to Life	$20.00	_____
_____	99 Days and a Get Up	9.95	_____
_____	99 Days to Re-Entry Success Journal (see page 124)	4.95	_____
_____	Best Jobs for Ex-Offenders	11.95	_____
_____	Best Resumes and Letters for Ex-Offenders	19.95	_____
_____	Beyond Bars	13.95	_____
_____	Chicken Soup for the Prisoner's Soul	14.95	_____
_____	Ex-Offender's Re-Entry Assistance Directory	29.95	_____
_____	Ex-Offender's Guide to a Responsible Life	15.95	_____
_____	Ex-Offender's Job Interview Guide	11.95	_____
_____	Ex-Offender's New Job Finding and Survival Guide (see page 124)	19.95	_____
_____	Ex-Offender's Quick Job Hunting Guide	11.95	_____
_____	Ex-Offender's Re-Entry Assistance Directory	29.95	_____
_____	Ex-Offender's Re-Entry Success Guide	11.95	_____
_____	Letters to an Incarcerated Brother	16.00	_____
_____	Life Beyond Loss	20.00	_____
_____	Picking Up the Pieces (for Women)	20.00	_____
_____	Quick Job Search for Ex-Offenders	7.95	_____
Attitude, Motivation, and Inspiration			
_____	7 Habits of Highly Effective People	$17.00	_____
_____	100 Ways to Motivate Yourself	15.99	_____

_____	Attitude Is Everything	$16.99 _____
_____	Awaken the Giant Within	17.99 _____
_____	Bouncing Back: Rewiring Your Brain	17.95 _____
_____	Change Your Thinking, Change Your Life	22.00 _____
_____	The Element: How Finding Your Passion Changes Everything	16.00 _____
_____	Finding Your Own North Star	15.00 _____
_____	Free At Last: Daily Meditations By and For Ex-Offenders	15.95 _____
_____	Goals!	19.95 _____
_____	Making Hope Happen	26.00 _____
_____	The Power of Habit	16.00 _____
_____	The Success Principles	18.99 _____
_____	What Should I Do With My Life?	16.00 _____

Reimagining Your Life With Purpose

_____	Life Reimagined: Discovering Your New Life Possibilities	$16.95 _____
_____	Man's Search for Meaning	9.99 _____
_____	The Power of Purpose	17.95 _____
_____	Repacking Your Bags	17.95 _____
_____	Something to Live For	16.95 _____
_____	Work Reimagined; Uncover Your Calling	16.95 _____

Career Exploration

_____	50 Best Jobs for Your Personality	$17.95 _____
_____	150 Best Jobs for a Secure Future	17.95 _____
_____	200 Best Jobs Through Apprenticeships	24.95 _____
_____	300 Best Jobs Without a Four-Year Degree	18.95 _____
_____	Occupational Outlook Handbook	19.95 _____

Finding Jobs and Getting Hired

_____	The 2-Hour Job Search	$12.99 _____
_____	Guerrilla Marketing for Job Hunters 3.0	21.95 _____
_____	Job Hunting Tips for People With Hot and Not-So-Hot Backgrounds	17.95 _____
_____	Knock 'Em Dead: The Ultimate Job Search Guide	16.99 _____
_____	No One Will Hire Me!	15.95 _____
_____	Overcoming Barriers to Employment	17.95 _____
_____	The Quick 30/30 Job Solution	14.95 _____
_____	Unemployed, But Moving On!	13.95 _____
_____	What Color is Your Parachute? (annual edition)	18.99 _____

Career Assessment

_____	Discover What You're Best At	$15.99 _____
_____	Do What You Are	18.99 _____
_____	Everything Career Tests Book	15.99 _____
_____	I Want to Do Something Else, But I'm Not Sure What It Is	15.95 _____
_____	Pathfinder	17.95 _____

Resumes and Cover Letters

_____	Best KeyWords for Resumes, Cover Letters, and Interviews	$17.95 _____
_____	Best Resumes for People Without a Four-Year Degree	19.95 _____
_____	Blue-Collar Resume and Job Hunting Guide	15.95 _____
_____	Resumes for Dummies	18.99 _____

Networking and Social Media

_____	How to Find a Job on LinkedIn, Facebook, Twitter, and Google+	$20.00 _____
_____	Job Searching With Social Media for Dummies	19.99 _____
_____	Knock 'Em Dead Social Networking	15.99 _____

Interviewing

_____	Best Answers to 202 Job Interview Questions	17.95 _____
_____	I Can't Believe They Asked Me That!	17.95 _____
_____	Job Interview Tips for People With Not-So-Hot Backgrounds	14.95 _____
_____	Job Interview for Dummies	17.99 _____
_____	Win the Interview, Win the Job	15.95 _____
_____	You Should Hire Me!	15.95 _____

Special Value Kits

_____	72 Re-Entry Success Books for Ex-Offenders	$1,179.95 _____
_____	Learning From Successes and Failures Kit	1,059.95 _____
_____	New Attitudes, Goals, and Motivations Kit	411.95 _____
_____	Overcoming Self-Defeating Behaviors and Bouncing Back Kit	245.95 _____
_____	Reimagining Life: Discovering Your Meaning and Purpose in Life Kit	203.95 _____
_____	Start Your Own Business Kit	316.95 _____

Survival and Re-Entry Curriculum Programs

_____	99 Days and a Get Up Training Program	$2,500.00 _____
_____	Life Without a Crutch Training Program	995.00 _____
_____	Map Through the Maze Program	389.95 _____
_____	A New Direction for Ex-Offenders: A Curriculum	4,695.00 _____
_____	Ultimate Re-Entry Success Curriculum Starter Kit	1,795.00 _____

Re-Entry and Survival DVDs

_____	9 to 5 Beats Ten to Life	$95.00 _____
_____	Breaking and Entering...Into a Better Life	199.95 _____
_____	Countdown to Freedom (for men or women)	695.00 _____
_____	Down But Not Out	149.00 _____
_____	Ex-Offender's Guide to Job Fair Success	129.00 _____
_____	From Prison to Home	`169.95 _____
_____	From Parole to Payroll (3 DVDs)	299.85 _____
_____	Life After Prison	99.95 _____
_____	Living Free	149.00 _____
_____	Parole: Getting Out and Staying Out	69.95 _____
_____	Putting the Bars Behind You	99.00 _____
_____	Starting Fresh With a Troubled Background Series	299.95 _____
_____	Stop Recidivism, Now! (3 DVDs)	275.00 _____

TERMS: Individuals must prepay; approved accounts are billed net 30 days. All orders under $100.00 should be prepaid.

RUSH ORDERS: fax, call, or email for more information on any special shipping arrangements and charges.

SUBTOTAL	_____
Virginia residents add 6% sales tax	_____
California residents add ___% sales tax	_____
Shipping ($5 +8% of SUBTOTAL)	_____
TOTAL ORDER	_____

Bill To:

Name_____ Title _____
Address _____
City _____ State/Zip _____
Phone ( )_____ (daytime)
Email _____

Ship To: (if different from "Bill To;" include street delivery address) :

Name_____ Title _____
Address _____
City _____ State/Zip _____
Phone ( )_____ (daytime)
Email _____

PAYMENT METHOD: ❑ **Purchase Order #_____** *(attach or fax with this order form)*

❑ **Check** – Make payable to IMPACT PUBLICATIONS

❑ **Credit Card**: ❑ Visa ❑ MasterCard ❑ AMEX ❑ Discover

Card #														Expiration Date		
Signature							Name on Card (print)